MW00852721

California
Wine
Winners

1994

Results of the 1993 Wine Judgings

Edited by
TRUDY AHLSTROM
and
J.T. DEVINE

ISBN 1-881796-00-0
ISSN 0883-4423

To order additional copies of this book or copies
of any of the previous ten editions, please send:
$8.75 for the 1993, 1992 or 1991 results;
$7.75 for the results of any years between 1983 and 1990.

VARIETAL FAIR
4022 Harrison Grade Road
Sebastopol, CA 95472
707 • 874 • 3105

TABLE OF CONTENTS

This is a simple report of all the medals awarded to California wines in this year's round of wine judgings. Take a look at the inside front cover to see what competitions we cover and how to read the front section. The book covers the 18 most popular varietals, as listed in the Table of Contents.

ORGANIZATION

The first section lists the award winners under specific varietals. Each varietal section is subdivided into groups of nine award winners, eight award winners, seven award winners, etc. The wines are listed alphabetically within these subdivisions, and identified by vintage, appellation and price. Across from each wine a Σ (double gold or special award) G (gold), S (silver), or B (bronze) shows what award was won in each of the competitions.

Johannisberg Riesling, Gewurztraminer and Sparkling wines are further broken down into residual sugar classes, and higher residual sugar wines have their "R.S." noted.

The second part of the book is an alphabetical listing of all the winning wineries, including their addresses. The inside back cover has a key to these listings. Under each winery, the winning wines are listed with the number of awards indicated in parentheses so they can be easily found in the front to see exactly what the medals are. Single-medal winners are listed only in the back, with the award and competition identified.

COMPETITIONS

The competitions start in January and end in July. Since many of the judgings have specific entry requirements (see pages 6 and 7) for the amount of wine to be available at the time of the judging or their fair, many wines entered in the early judgings are too sold out to be entered in the later ones. Keep your copies of this book to compare awards in previous/subsequent years.

The statistics charts will also show you how many of the entered wines win medals in each competition, and how many are gold-plus, gold, silver and bronze. Since this book only covers wines from California, the charts show how many of the total medals were for California wines. And since we don't include every varietal judged (no Gamay, Grenache, Port, etc.) we also list the number of awards from each judging that actually appear in this book.

Some smaller wineries don't enter because of the expense. It is not just the entry fee and paperwork, but also the wine they must give to the competitions if they win. Many of these small producers sell out all their wines every year anyhow. On the other hand, we have seen the ones who choose to compete enter a period of growth and recognition just in the way their medals suggest they should.

On exactly the opposite side are the larger, older wineries who feel they don't need to compete to prove their worth.

We are prohibited not as much by space limitations as by access to information from publishing a list of all the wines entered that did not win a medal. For those reasons, this book cannot be a complete list of who won and who did not win.

POINT COUNTS & REGION COMPARISONS

The first page of each varietal section ranks the top dozen or so winners by weighting the value of each award. Double Golds, Sweepstakes, Best of Class, and other special merit awards = 7 points. (We do not include the best of region and best of region varietal awards from the State Fair for these). Gold = 5 points, Silver = 3 points, and Bronze = 1. The values are arbitrary; it is just another way of looking at the awards.

Also included is a graph that shows which regions of the state took how many points of those weighted medals. The regions refer to those areas where the grapes were grown, not necessarily where the wineries are located:

North Coast ....Lake, Mendocino, Marin and Solano Co.
Sonoma ....Sonoma County (11 Appellations).
Napa ....Napa County (5 Appellations).
Bay Area ....Alameda, Contra Costa, San Mateo, Santa
...................................Clara and Santa Cruz Co.
No. Central Coast ....Monterey and San Benito Counties.
So. Central Coast .....San Luis Obispo and Santa Barbara Co.
South Coast...............L.A., Orange, Riverside, San Diego
...................................and Ventura Counties.
Sierra Foothills ....Amador, Calaveras, El Dorado, Mariposa,
...................................Nevada, Placer, Tuolomne, Yuba Co.
Other ....All other California Counties
California ....Non-specified blends from above
...................................appellations.

COMPETITIONS	ENTRIES # Wines #Wineries # in Calif.	MEDALS Total # From CA In book	AWARDS Σ G S B
LOS ANGELES COUNTY FAIR P. O. Box 2250 Pomona, CA 91769 (909) 623-3111	1698 348 296	496 424 363	13 71 120 156
ORANGE COUNTY FAIR P. O. Box 11059 Costa Mesa, CA 92627 (714) 546-8664	2589 ? ?	806 806 552	6 119 211 313
FARMERS FAIR, RIVERSIDE 18700 Lake Perris Drive Perris, CA 92571 (909) 657-4221	1500 450 ?	556 476 399	19 40 133 236
SAN FRANCISCO FAIR 455 Golden Gate Avenue #2095 San Francisco, CA 94102 (415) 703-2729	1891 430 341	596 481 419	13 35 131 239
DALLAS MORNING NEWS P. O. Box 38643 Dallas, TX 75238 (214) 319-7000	1306 325 ?	458 319 284	0 37 92 155
CALIFORNIA STATE FAIR P. O. Box 15649 Sacramento, CA 95852 (916) 263-3159	1845 408 408	774 774 646	11 79 224 332
NEW WORLD INTERNATIONAL 305 Sacramento Place Ontario, CA 91764 (909) 391-1015, Ext. 31	1450 321 247	587 453 411	21 83 140 166
RENO-WEST COAST COMP. P. O. Box 837 Reno, NV 89504 (702) 827-7618	1291 277 247	470 427 389	14 49 128 199
SAN DIEGO COMPETITION P. O. Box 880881 San Diego, CA 92168 (619) 421-9463	1809 408 ?	675 538 471	13 43 128 286

1994 Entry Deadline Judging Dates	ENTRY Fee Bottles to Send Min. Produced Min. Inventory at judging	WINNERS Require- ments after Judging	JUDGING SCOPE Geographic Area Covered Judging Categories Entry Restrictions
LOS ANGELES June 15 Mid-July	$25.00 Six 120 Gal. "Some"	Golds only to sell 2-3 cs. to fair	Any wine from any of the Ameri- can continents. Some judged in vintage groups. Limit of one entry per class.
ORANGE CO. May 1 End of May	No charge Six None "Some"	All winners invited to pour at the fair	California wines available in Orange Co. Judged in price categories. Not all entries voluntary.Current releases only.
RIVERSIDE March 25 April 30-May 1	$25.00 Four 500 Gal 50 Cases	All entries invited to pour at the fair	Any U. S. wine. Some judged in vintage groups. Chards judged in style groups.
SAN FRAN. May June	$45.00 Four None "Some"	GG & some G invited to pour at the fair	Any U.S. wine. No limit on number of entries.
DALLAS Dec. 10 Jan 8 & 9	$55.00 Four 120 Gal. 3 Cases	Golds to give 3 cases for tastings	Any U. S. wine. Limit of 3 entries per category.
STATE FAIR Mid-June Mid-July	$25.00 Six 300 Gal. 125 Cases	Golds to sell up to 5 cases for the fair	All California wine. Wines judged in 10 geogrphical groups. Limit of 2 entries per class per region.
NEW WORLD Jan 28 Feb. 17 & 18	$35.00 Six None None	All entries invited to pour at awards	Any wine from the New World. All wines judged in price groups.
WEST COAST Early April Early May	$17.00 Six 500 Gal. 150 Cases	Golds are required to pour at events	Wines from California, Idaho, Oregon and Washington. Some grouped in vintage/price. No limit on number of entries.
SAN DIEGO April 4 April 23 & 24	$25.00 Four 300 Gal. No minimum	All winners to donate 1 case for charity sale	Any U. S. vinifera wine. Some judged in vintage groups. No limit on number of entries, except same wine in 2 classes.

EST. 1858

GUNDLACH BUNDSCHU

Estate Bottled

1990

RHINEFARM VINEYARDS

SONOMA VALLEY
CABERNET FRANC

PRODUCED AND BOTTLED BY
GUNDLACH BUNDSCHU WINERY B.W. 64
VINEBURG, CALIFORNIA 95487
ALCOHOL 13.4% BY VOLUME

Graeser

1989

Napa Valley

ESTATE BOTTLED

PRODUCED AND BOTTLED BY
RICHARD L. GRAESER WINERY   CALISTOGA, CA.
ALCOHOL 13.0% BY VOLUME   CONTAINS SULFITES

Cabernet Franc

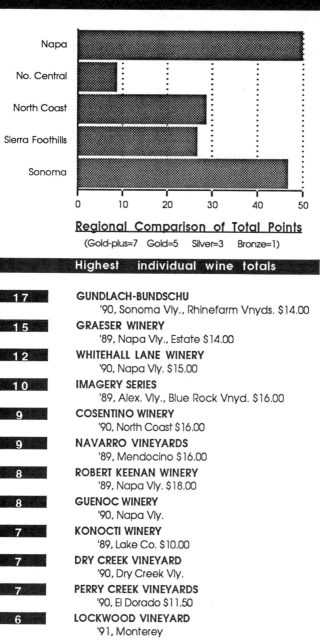

Regional Comparison of Total Points

(Gold-plus=7   Gold=5   Silver=3   Bronze=1)

Highest individual wine totals

17   **GUNDLACH-BUNDSCHU**
'90, Sonoma Vly., Rhinefarm Vnyds. $14.00

15   **GRAESER WINERY**
'89, Napa Vly., Estate $14.00

12   **WHITEHALL LANE WINERY**
'90, Napa Vly. $15.00

10   **IMAGERY SERIES**
'89, Alex. Vly., Blue Rock Vnyd. $16.00

9   **COSENTINO WINERY**
'90, North Coast $16.00

9   **NAVARRO VINEYARDS**
'89, Mendocino $16.00

8   **ROBERT KEENAN WINERY**
'89, Napa Vly. $18.00

8   **GUENOC WINERY**
'90, Napa Vly.

7   **KONOCTI WINERY**
'89, Lake Co. $10.00

7   **DRY CREEK VINEYARD**
'90, Dry Creek Vly.

7   **PERRY CREEK VINEYARDS**
'90, El Dorado $11.50

6   **LOCKWOOD VINEYARD**
'91, Monterey

Cabernet Franc

	L.A.	Orange	Farmers	San Fran	Dallas	State Fair	New World	W. Coast	San Diego
5 AWARDS									
GRAESER WINERY '89, Napa Vly., Estate $14.00	G	B	S			G			B
GUNDLACH-BUNDSCHU '90, Sonoma Vly., Rhinefarm Vnyds. $14.00	G	B					S	S	G
KONOCTI WINERY '89, Lake Co. $10.00		B	B	B			B		S
4 AWARDS									
GEYSER PEAK WINERY '89, Alexander Vly. $9.00				B	S		G		B
ROBERT KEENAN WINERY '89, Napa Vly. $18.00				S		B	S		B
WHITEHALL LANE WINERY '90, Napa Vly. $15.00				S	S	G	B		
3 AWARDS									
COSENTINO WINERY '91, North Coast $18.00	B	B		B					
COSENTINO WINERY '90, North Coast $16.00		B					Σ		B
DRY CREEK VINEYARD '90, Dry Creek Vly.	B					B	G		
GRANITE SPRINGS WINERY '90, El Dorado, Estate $12.50			S			B	B		
NAVARRO VINEYARDS '89, Mendocino $16.00			Σ			B	B		
NEVADA CITY WINERY 'NV, Sierra Foothills $12.00		B	B				S		
PERRY CREEK VINEYARDS '90, El Dorado $11.50		B				G		B	
SEBASTIANI VINEYARDS '89, Sonoma Co., Family Selection $9.00						B	S		B
2 AWARDS									
GUENOC WINERY '90, Napa Vly.	S					G			
IMAGERY SERIES '89, Alex. Vly., Blue Rock Vnyd. $16.00	Σ						S		
LOCKWOOD VINEYARD '91, Monterey	S					S			

L.A. Orange Farmers	San Fran Dallas	State Fair	New World W. Coast San Diego	Cabernet Franc
	B		B	**MADRONA VINEYARDS** '89, El Dorado $11.00
B B				**V. SATTUI WINERY** '90, Napa Vly., Rosen Brand Vnyd.

2 AWARDS

1989

Chateau St. Jean

SONOMA COUNTY

Cabernet Sauvignon

PRODUCED AND BOTTLED BY
CHATEAU ST. JEAN • KENWOOD, CALIFORNIA, USA
BONDED WINERY NO. 4710 • TABLE WINE

GARY FARRELL

1990
LADI'S VINEYARD
SONOMA COUNTY
CABERNET SAUVIGNON

PRODUCED AND BOTTLED BY GARY FARRELL
HEALDSBURG CA. CONTAINS SULFITES. TABLE WINE

Cabernet Sauvignon

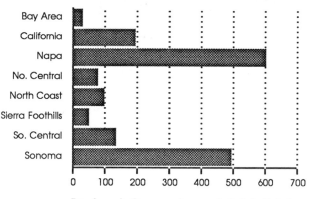

Regional Comparison of Total Points
(Gold-plus=7 Gold=5 Silver=3 Bronze=1)

Highest individual wine totals

29 **CHATEAU ST. JEAN**
'89, Sonoma Co. $18.00

27 **GARY FARRELL WINES**
'90, Sonoma Co., Ladi's Vnyd. $18.00

21 **VILLA MT. EDEN WINERY**
'89, Napa Vly., Grand Reserve $15.00

20 **CRESTON VINEYARDS**
'89, Paso Robles $10.00

19 **A. RAFANELLI WINERY**
'90, Dry Creek Vly., Unfiltered $15.00

19 **J. LOHR WINERY**
'90, Paso Robles, Seven Oaks $12.25

18 **FETZER VINEYARDS**
'87, Sonoma Co., Reserve $22.00

17 **CONN CREEK WINERY**
'88, Napa Vly., Barrel Sel. $16.00

16 **BENZIGER WINERY**
'90, Sonoma Co. $12.50

16 **HUSCH VINEYARDS**
'89, Mendocino, North Field Sel. $18.00

16 **WINDSOR VINEYARDS**
'89, Sonoma Co., Signature Series $18.00

Cabernet Sauvignon	L.A.	Orange Farmers	San Fran	Dallas	State Fair	New World	W. Coast	San Diego
9 AWARDS								
CHATEAU ST. JEAN '89, Sonoma Co. $18.00	S	G S	B	G	B	S	G	S
7 AWARDS								
BAREFOOT CELLARS 'NV, California $4.00	B	B		B	S	S	B	G
CONN CREEK WINERY '88, Napa Vly., Barrel Sel. $16.00	S	G	S	B	S		B	B
GARY FARRELL WINES '90, Sonoma Co., Ladi's Vnyd. $18.00	S	G	G	S	S	G	S	
ZD WINES '90, Napa Vly. $20.00	S	B S	B	B		B		G
6 AWARDS								
BENZIGER WINERY '90, Sonoma Co. $12.50	B	B Σ			B		S	S
CONN CREEK WINERY '89, Napa Vly., Reserve $23.00	S	S	B		S	S	B	
CRESTON VINEYARDS '89, Paso Robles $10.00		S	S	S	G	G		B
GOLDEN CREEK VINEYARD '90, Sonoma Co. $12.00		B		S	B	B	B	B
NAPA RIDGE '89, North Coast, Reserve $12.00	S	B	B		S		S	B
SEQUOIA GROVE VINEYARDS '89, Napa Vly. $16.00	B			B	B	Σ	B	B
5 AWARDS								
ADELAIDA CELLARS '89, Paso Robles $16.25	B	S		B		S		B
DE LOACH VINEYARDS '90, Russian River Vly., Estate $16.00		S	B	G		S		B
DRY CREEK VINEYARD '90, Dry Creek Vly. $14.00		S B	B	B				B
FETZER VINEYARDS '90, California, Valley Oaks $8.00		G B		S		S	B	
FOREST GLEN WINERY '90, Sonoma Co., Barrel Select $12.00		B	B	G		S	B	
GEYSER PEAK WINERY '90, Alexander Vly., Reserve $15.00		S	B	B	B		S	
GRGICH HILLS CELLAR '87, Napa Vly. $30.00	S	S			B		S	B

Cabernet Sauvignon

L.A.	Orange	Farmers	San Fran	Dallas	State Fair	New World	W. Coast	San Diego	
5 AWARDS									
B	S		G	B				G	**HOP KILN WINERY** '90, Russian River Vly. $14.00
B	B		S				G	B	**KENWOOD VINEYARDS** '89, Sonoma Vly., Jack London $20.00
B			G			B	B	B	**LOUIS M. MARTINI WINERY** '89, Sonoma, Monte Rosso Vnyd. $22.00
B			S		S		S	B	**MAZZOCCO VINEYARDS** '89, Sonoma Co. $15.00
B				B	S	B	G		**MONTICELLO CELLARS** '89, Napa Vly., Corley Reserve $25.00
S	Σ	S		B	G				**A. RAFANELLI WINERY** '90, Dry Creek Vly., Unfiltered $15.00
B			S		S		S	B	**SILVERADO VINEYARDS** '90, Stags Leap Dist. $16.50
B			B			B	G	S	**SWANSON VINEYARDS** '89, Napa Vly. $23.00
S	S	B	S				B		**VILLA MT. EDEN WINERY** '90, California, Cellar Select $10.00
S	S	S	S					G	**VILLA MT. EDEN WINERY** '89, Napa Vly., Grand Reserve $15.00
4 AWARDS									
B					B	B	B		**ADELAIDA CELLARS** '90, San Luis Obispo $17.00
	G				B	B	B		**BEL ARBORS** '90, California, Founder's Sel. $6.75
B						B	S	B	**BON MARCHE** '91, Sonoma Co. $8.00
B				B		Σ			**BRAREN PAULI WINERY** '90, Dry Creek Vly. $13.00
S			B	B		B			**DAVID BRUCE WINERY** '90, Mendocino, Reserve, Select $18.00
B			B	B		S			**BURGESS CELLARS** '89, Napa Vly. $18.00
S			B			S	B		**CALLAWAY VINEYARD** '90, California $10.00
S	S			B		S			**CANYON ROAD CELLARS** '91, California $4.75

Cabernet Sauvignon

4 AWARDS

Winery	L.A.	Orange Farmers	San Fran	Dallas	State Fair	New World	W. Coast	San Diego
EVEREST '89, Dry Creek Vly. $15.00			B			S	B	S
FETZER VINEYARDS '89, California, Barrel Select $11.00		B		B	S		G	
FETZER VINEYARDS '87, Sonoma Co., Reserve $22.00	G	S	S				Σ	
GUENOC WINERY '90, Napa, Beckstoffer, Reserve $35.00	B	G	B				B	
HUSCH VINEYARDS '89, Mendocino, North Field Sel. $18.00			S		G		G	S
JOULLIAN VINEYARD '89, Carmel Vly. $14.00			S		S		S	B
LAVA CAP WINERY '89, El Dorado, Estate $13.00	B	S	B					S
MENDOCINO HILLS '89, Mendocino Co. $18.00	B		S		S		B	
MOUNT VEEDER WINERY '89, Napa Vly. $21.50	S	S					B	B
MURPHY-GOODE WINERY '90, Alexander Vly., Murphy Ranch $15.00		B		B	B			Σ
NAVARRO VINEYARDS '88, Mendocino $16.00	G	S	B				B	
RAYMOND VINEYARD '89, Napa Vly. $15.00		B	B	G				S
V. SATTUI WINERY '88, Napa Vly. $14.75	B		B			B		B
SEBASTIANI VINEYARDS '88, Sonoma Co., Reserve $14.00	B	B	B		G			
SHAFER VINEYARDS '90, Napa Vly., Stag's Leap Dist. $19.00		B				G	S	G
ST. CLEMENT VINEYARDS '90, Napa Vly. $20.00	G				B	B	G	
SYLVESTER VINEYARDS '88, Paso Robles, Kiara Reserve $9.00		B				B	B	
WINDSOR VINEYARDS '89, Sonoma Co., Signature Series $18.00	S		G				G	

3 AWARDS

Winery	L.A.	Orange Farmers	San Fran	Dallas	State Fair	New World	W. Coast	San Diego
AUDUBON CELLARS '91, Napa Vly., Oakville Ranch $11.00		B		B	G			

Cabernet Sauvignon

L.A.	Orange Farmers	San Fran	Dallas	State Fair	New World	W. Coast	San Diego	
3 AWARDS								
B	B				B			**BEAULIEU VINEYARD** '90, Napa Vly., Rutherford, Estate $13.00
B			B		B			**BERINGER VINEYARDS** '87, Napa Vly., Chabot Vnyd. $32.00
				S	B	B		**CHATEAU SOUVERAIN** '89, Alexander Vly. $10.50
		B	B		B			**CHATEAU SOUVERAIN** '88, Alexander Vly., Reserve $13.00
	S		B		B			**CLOS DU BOIS** '90, Alexander Vly. $12.75
			B		G	S		**CLOS DU VAL** '89, Napa Vly., Stags Leap Dist. $18.00
		B		B	S			**CORBETT CANYON VINEYARDS** '91, California, Coastal Classic $8.00
S	B				B			**COSENTINO WINERY** '90, Napa Vly. $16.00
		B		S		S		**FETZER VINEYARDS** '91, California, Valley Oaks $8.00
S				B	B			**FIRESTONE VINEYARD** '90, Santa Ynez Vly. $12.00
B		B			S			**GEYSER PEAK WINERY** '90, Sonoma Co. $9.00
	B				G	S		**GUNDLACH-BUNDSCHU** '90, Sonoma Vly., Rhinefarm Vnyds. $15.00
G	G				B			**HUSCH VINEYARDS** '89, Mendocino, La Ribera Vnyds. $14.00
B		S		B				**INDIAN SPRINGS VINEYARDS** '89, Sierra Foothills $10.00
		S		B		S		**KATHRYN KENNEDY WINERY** '89, Santa Cruz Mtns. $54.00
B		S				S		**CHARLES KRUG WINERY** '89, Napa Vly., Estate $12.00
	S			S			Σ	**LOCKWOOD VINEYARD** '91, Monterey Co. $10.00
				Σ	G		Σ	**J. LOHR WINERY** '90, Paso Robles, Seven Oaks $12.25
B	B				B			**PAUL MASSON VINEYARDS** '88, Monterey Co. $8.00

3 AWARDS

	L.A.	Orange Farmers	San Fran	Dallas	State Fair	New World	W. Coast	San Diego
MIRASSOU VINEYARDS '90, Monterey Co., Reserve $12.00		G				G		S
MONTEREY VINEYARD '91, Monterey Co., Classic $6.00	S	B			B			
NEWLAN VINEYARDS '87, Napa Vly. $15.00	B		B	S				
J. PEDRONCELLI WINERY '86, Dry Creek Vly., Reserve $14.00	S		B	G				
PEJU PROVINCE '89, Napa Vly., HB Vnyd. $30.00	S				S			S
PERRY CREEK VINEYARDS '90, El Dorado Co.					G		B	B
RAYMOND VINEYARD '87, Napa Vly., Reserve $25.00		B					S	B
ROYCE VINEYARDS '89, Napa Vly.					S	B		B
V. SATTUI WINERY '89, Napa Vly., Suzanne's Vnyd. $15.00			S	B		B		
V. SATTUI WINERY '88, Napa Vly., Preston, Reserve $35.00				B		B		B
SEBASTIANI VINEYARDS '89, Sonoma Series $9.00		G	B	S				
SEBASTIANI VINEYARDS '89, Sonoma Vly., Cherryblock	B			B		B		
SEQUOIA GROVE VINEYARDS '90, Napa Vly., Estate Reserve $25.00				S	B			B
SONOMA CREEK WINERY '90, Sonoma Vly. $10.00					G	S		B
ST. CLEMENT VINEYARDS '89, Napa Vly. $20.00		S	S			S		
ST. SUPERY WINERY '89, Napa Vly., Dollarhide Ranch					B	B		B
RODNEY STRONG VINEYARDS '90, Sonoma Co. $10.00		S	B	B				
SUNRISE '88, Santa Cruz Mtns. $15.00	S		B	S				
SWANSON VINEYARDS '88, Napa Vly. $23.00	B	G		B				

L.A.	Orange Farmers	San Fran	Dallas	State Fair	New World	W. Coast	San Diego	Cabernet Sauvignon
					3 AWARDS			
		B				S	S	**VENDANGE** '91, California $6.00
B		G				G		**VICHON WINERY** '90, Napa Vly.
S		B	Σ					**VICHON WINERY** '89, Stags Leap Dist. $24.00
B						S	B	**VINA VISTA WINERY** '88, Alexander Vly. $12.00
		B				G	S	**WEIBEL VINEYARDS** '89, Mendocino, Reserve $8.00
S				S		B		**WINDSOR VINEYARDS** '90, Mendocino Co., Reserve $14.50
B		S					B	**YORK MOUNTAIN WINERY** '87, San Luis Obispo Co.
					2 AWARDS			
		B					B	**ARCIERO WINERY** '89, Paso Robles
			S		S			**AUDUBON CELLARS** '90, Napa Vly. $11.00
			B	S				**BANDIERA WINERY** '89, Napa Vly. $7.00
B				B				**BARON HERZOG WINE CELLARS** '91, California $12.00
B	B							**BEAULIEU VINEYARD** '88, Napa Vly., Latour Reserve $37.00
				S		S		**BERINGER VINEYARDS** '89, Napa Vly., Reserve $45.00
					S	B		**BERINGER VINEYARDS** '88, Napa Vly., Chabot Vnyd. $35.00
B	B							**BLACK MOUNTAIN VINEYARD** '90, Alexander Vly., Fat Cat $18.00
		S				B		**BOEGER WINERY** '89, El Dorado
B		G						**BRAREN PAULI WINERY** '89, Dry Creek Vly., Mauritson Vnyd. $13.00
B					B			**BUENA VISTA WINERY** '90, Carneros $11.00

19

Cabernet Sauvignon

	L.A.	Orange	Farmers	San Fran	Dallas	State Fair	New World	W. Coast	San Diego
2 AWARDS									
CARMENET '91, Sonoma Vly., Dynamite $15.00			B	B					
CASTORO CELLARS '90, Paso Robles, Reserve $13.00		G						S	
CASTORO CELLARS '90, Paso Robles $10.00				B	B				
CAYMUS VINEYARDS '90, California, Vintner Select	S						B		
CAYMUS VINEYARDS '89, Napa Vly. $24.00						B	G		
CHALK HILL WINERY '90, Chalk Hill, Estate						G			B
CHATEAU JULIEN WINERY '89, Monterey Co., Reserve $13.00				Σ			G		
CHATEAU SOUVERAIN '90, Alexander Vly. $11.00				S					S
CHATOM VINEYARDS '90, Calaveras Co. $14.00	S	S							
CHESTNUT HILL '90, California, Coastal Cuvee						B			B
CHIMNEY ROCK '89, Napa Vly., Stag's Leap Dist. $18.00				S					B
CLONINGER CELLARS '90, Monterey Co. $15.00				B					B
COSENTINO WINERY '88, North Coast, Reserve $25.00	S	S							
CRESTON VINEYARDS '89, Paso Robles, Winemakers Sel. $17.00				G		S			
DEER VALLEY VINEYARDS '90, Monterey Co. $6.00		B							B
DEER VALLEY VINEYARDS '89, Monterey Co. $6.00						B	S		
DOMAINE ST. GEORGE WINERY '88, Alexander Vly., Cuvee, Res, $8.50	S	G							
J. PATRICK DORE WINES '91, California $5.00		B						B	
EBERLE WINERY '89, Paso Robles, Estate						S	B		

20

2 AWARDS

L.A.	Orange Farmers	San Fran	Dallas	State Fair	New World	W. Coast	San Diego	
B					S			**ESTANCIA WINERY** '90, Alexander Vly. $10.00
B					B			**ESTRELLA RIVER** '90, California, Prop. Reserve $6.00
		B	B					**FETZER VINEYARDS** '86, Sonoma Co., Reserve $22.00
	S			S				**FLORA SPRINGS** '89, Napa, Reserve $38.00
B					B			**GARLAND RANCH** '91, California $7.00
			B	B				**GRAND CRU VINEYARDS** '90, California, Premium Selection $8.00
		G	S					**GUENOC WINERY** '89, Napa, Beckstoffer Reserve $30.00
			S	S				**GUGLIELMO WINERY** '86, Santa Clara Vly., Reserve $12.00
				Σ	B			**HESS COLLECTION** '89, Napa Vly. $16.25
B	B							**HUSCH VINEYARDS** '90, Mendocino, La Ribera Vnyd. $14.00
S	S							**KENDALL-JACKSON WINERY** '90, California, Vintner's Reserve
S					G			**KENDALL-JACKSON WINERY** '88, Calif., Grand Reserve $30.00
	S	Σ						**KENWOOD VINEYARDS** '89, Sonoma Vly. $15.00
	B				B			**LATCHAM VINEYARDS** '90, El Dorado $12.00
	S		S					**LIPARITA** '90, Napa, Howell Mtn. $35.00
B	B							**M. MARION** '91, Napa Vly.
G	G							**MARKHAM VINEYARDS** '89, Napa Vly. $14.00
			B		S			**LOUIS M. MARTINI WINERY** '89, Napa Vly., Reserve $14.00
	B				B			**MERIDIAN VINEYARDS** '90, Paso Robles $13.00

Cabernet Sauvignon

	L.A.	Orange	Farmers	San Fran	Dallas	State Fair	New World	W. Coast	San Diego
2 AWARDS									
MONTEVINA WINES '90, California						B	S		
MONTPELLIER VINEYARDS '90, California $8.00		B					S		
MORGAN '89, Carmel Vly. $18.00						S			B
NAPA RIDGE '90, Central Coast $7.50		B					Σ		
OAKVILLE RANCH VINEYARDS '90, Napa Vly. $27.00			G	S					
PEJU PROVINCE '90, Napa Vly., HB Vnyd. $30.00					B			S	
JOSEPH PHELPS VINEYARDS '90, Napa Vly. $18.00	S				S				
R. H. PHILLIP VINEYARD '91, California $8.00			S		B				
RANCHO SISQUOC '89, Santa Maria Vly. $14.00	B	B							
RAYMOND VINEYARD '88, Napa Vly., Reserve $25.00	G				B				
RUTHERFORD HILL WINERY '84, Napa, Library Reserve $23.00	S			S					
SEQUOIA GROVE VINEYARDS '90, Napa Vly, Estate $16.00							B	G	
SILVER CANYON '89, Paso Robles						B	B		
SILVER RIDGE VINEYARDS '89, Napa Vly.						B			B
SONOMA CREEK WINERY '91, Sonoma Co. $10.00			S	S					
ST. FRANCIS WINERY '89, Sonoma Vly., Reserve $24.00			S					Σ	
STAG'S LEAP WINE CELLARS '90, Napa Vly. $18.00			B						S
STELTZNER VINEYARDS '88, Napa Vly.	B							B	
STEVENOT WINERY '89, Calaveras Co., Reserve						Σ			S

L.A. Orange Farmers	San Fran Dallas State Fair	New World W. Coast San Diego	Cabernet Sauvignon
		2 AWARDS	
	B	B	**TITUS** '90, Napa Vly. $20.00
	S	G	**TULOCAY WINERY** '87, Napa Vly., Cliff Vnyd.
S B			**VALLEY OF THE MOON WINERY** '89, Sonoma Co. $9.00
	S	B	**VICHON WINERY** '90, Calif., Coastal Selection $9.00
S		B	**WENTE BROS.** '90, Livermore Vly., Estate $9.00
B		B	**WILLIAM WHEELER WINERY** '89, Dry Creek Vly. $12.50
S	S		**WHITEHALL LANE WINERY** '89, Napa Vly., Reserve
B		S	**WILD HORSE WINERY** '90, Paso Robles $12.00
	B	B	**J. WILE & SONS** '91, Napa Vly. $10.00
	B B		**WINDEMERE WINES** '90, Napa Vly., Diamond Mtn.
S		B	**WINDSOR VINEYARDS** '89, Sonoma Co. $10.00
B		B	**WINDSOR VINEYARDS** '88, North Coast $12.00
B	B		**WINDSOR VINEYARDS** '88, River West Vnyd., Estate $13.00
	S	G	**WINTERBROOK WINERY** '90, Napa Vly., Grand Reserve $15.00
		B G	**YORK MOUNTAIN WINERY** '88, San Luis Obispo Co. $12.00

BARREL FERMENTED

FOREST GLEN
1991 CALIFORNIA CHARDONNAY

ALC. 12.5% BY VOL.

Cambria

1990

RESERVE

CHARDONNAY

SANTA MARIA VALLEY

Chardonnay

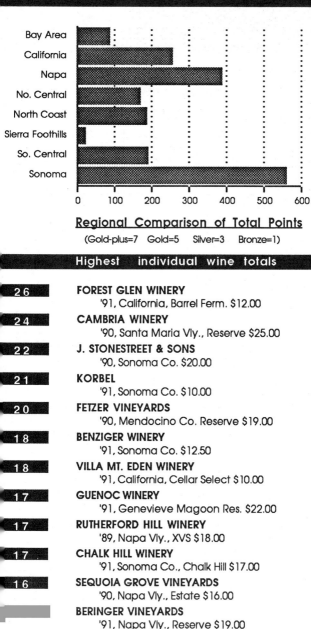

Regional Comparison of Total Points

(Gold-plus=7 Gold=5 Silver=3 Bronze=1)

Highest individual wine totals

26 **FOREST GLEN WINERY**
'91, California, Barrel Ferm. $12.00

24 **CAMBRIA WINERY**
'90, Santa Maria Vly., Reserve $25.00

22 **J. STONESTREET & SONS**
'90, Sonoma Co. $20.00

21 **KORBEL**
'91, Sonoma Co. $10.00

20 **FETZER VINEYARDS**
'90, Mendocino Co. Reserve $19.00

18 **BENZIGER WINERY**
'91, Sonoma Co. $12.50

18 **VILLA MT. EDEN WINERY**
'91, California, Cellar Select $10.00

17 **GUENOC WINERY**
'91, Genevieve Magoon Res. $22.00

17 **RUTHERFORD HILL WINERY**
'89, Napa Vly., XVS $18.00

17 **CHALK HILL WINERY**
'91, Sonoma Co., Chalk Hill $17.00

16 **SEQUOIA GROVE VINEYARDS**
'90, Napa Vly., Estate $16.00

BERINGER VINEYARDS
'91, Napa Vly., Reserve $19.00

Chardonnay	L.A.	Orange	Farmers	San Fran	Dallas	State Fair	New World	W. Coast	San Diego
8 AWARDS									
FOREST GLEN WINERY '91, California, Barrel Ferm. $12.00		B	S	G	S	S	S	S	C
7 AWARDS									
FETZER VINEYARDS '91, Mendocino, Barrel Sel. $11.00	B	B	S	G		B	B		▮
GLEN ELLEN WINERY '92, California, Prop. Reserve $6.00	S	B	B	S		G	B		▮
6 AWARDS									
BENZIGER WINERY '91, Sonoma Co. $12.50	Σ		B	S		S	S	B	
CAMBRIA WINERY '90, Santa Maria Vly., Reserve $25.00	G	S	Σ			B		S	C
CRICHTON HALL '91, Napa, Chardonnay Vnyd. $18.00	S	B		S	B	B			▮
FETZER VINEYARDS '90, Mendocino Co. Reserve $19.00	B				G	S	S	G	S
GRAND CRU VINEYARDS '91, California $8.00		B	S	B		B	S	S	
JOULLIAN VINEYARD '91, Monterey $10.50	S		B	B		B	G	S	
LANDMARK VINEYARDS '91, Sonoma Co., Overlook $12.00	G	B	B	S		B		B	
MAZZOCCO VINEYARDS '91, Sonoma Co., River Lane $15.00	B	S				S	B	S	
SEQUOIA GROVE VINEYARDS '90, Napa Vly., Estate $16.00			B	B	G	S	S	S	
SILVER RIDGE VINEYARDS '91, California, Barrel Ferm. $12.00		B	S			B	S	S	
J. STONESTREET & SONS '90, Sonoma Co. $20.00	S		S			S	G	B	
5 AWARDS									
BEL ARBORS '92, California, Founder's Sel. $7.00	S			B		B	S		
CASTORO CELLARS '92, San Luis Obispo Co. $9.50		G	S	S		S			
CHATEAU DE BAUN WINERY '91, Russian River Vly. $10.00		G		B	B	G		B	
GEYSER PEAK WINERY '91, Sonoma Co. $9.00	B	S	B			S	G		

L.A.	Orange Farmers	San Fran	Dallas	State Fair	New World	W. Coast	San Diego	Chardonnay
				5	AWARDS			
B	B	S	B				B	**GREENWOOD RIDGE VINEYARDS** '91, Mendocino Co. $16.00
Σ	S		G		B	B		**GUENOC WINERY** '91, Genevieve Magoon Res. $22.00
B	S	B	G				S	**GUNDLACH-BUNDSCHU** '91, Sangiacomo Ranch $14.00
B		S		S	B	B		**HANNA WINERY** '91, Sonoma Co. $13.50
S	Σ	S	B	B				**KENDALL-JACKSON WINERY** '91, Calif., Prop. Grand Reserve $23.00
	Σ	G	B			S	G	**KORBEL** '91, Sonoma Co. $10.00
B		S	G		B	B		**LEEWARD WINERY** '91, Central Coast $11.00
S	S	S	G		B			**MERIDIAN VINEYARDS** '91, Edna Vly. $14.00
		G	B	S	G		S	**RUTHERFORD HILL WINERY** '89, Napa Vly., XVS $18.00
B	G	B	B		G			**V. SATTUI WINERY** '91, Napa Vly., Carsi Vnyd., Estate $16.00
				4	AWARDS			
B	B		S	G				**ADELAIDA CELLARS** '91, San Luis Obispo Co. $17.00
S		B			Σ	B		**BARGETTO WINERY** '90, Santa Cruz Mtns. $14.00
	S	G		G			B	**BELVEDERE WINERY** '91, Sonoma, Preferred Stock $18.00
Σ			G		S	B		**BERINGER VINEYARDS** '91, Napa Vly., Reserve $19.00
B	S	B			S			**BUENA VISTA WINERY** '91, Carneros $11.00
		S	B	G	S			**DAVIS BYNUM WINERY** '91, Russian Riv., Allen-Griffin Vnyds. $17.00
		S		S		G	S	**BYRON VINEYARD** '91, Santa Barbara Co., Reserve $20.00
		S	S	S	B			**CAMBRIA WINERY** '91, Santa Maria, Katherine's Vnyd. $16.00

Chardonnay	L.A.	Orange	Farmers	San Fran	Dallas	State Fair	New World	W. Coast	San Diego
4 AWARDS									
CANYON ROAD CELLARS '92, California $4.75		B	B					B	G
COSENTINO WINERY '91, Napa Vly., The Sculptor $20.00		S	B			S		S	
DRY CREEK VINEYARD '91, Sonoma Co. $13.00	B	S		B				B	
DRY CREEK VINEYARD '90, Dry Creek Vly., Reserve $20.00	S					B	B		B
GLORIA FERRER '91, Carneros $15.00	B		S			B	G		
FRANCISCAN OAKVILLE ESTATE '91, Napa Vly., Cuvee Sauvage $24.00		G				B		S	B
FRANCISCAN OAKVILLE ESTATE '91, Napa Vly.						B	S	S	B
J. FRITZ WINERY '91, Sonoma Co. $9.50		B		S			B		B
J. FURST '91, California $9.00			G	S		B	B		
GAN EDEN '90, Alex. Vly./Mendocino, Res. $16.00			B	B		B	B		
GRGICH HILLS CELLAR '90, Napa Vly. $22.00			B		B		B		B
GUENOC WINERY '89, Genevieve Magoon Res. $22.00	B	S						B	B
HANDLEY CELLARS '90, Anderson Vly. $11.00	B				B		S	B	
KONOCTI WINERY '92, Lake Co. $9.00				B	B			B	B
LAURIER '89, Sonoma Co. $15.00		S		B			B		G
LAVA CAP WINERY '91, El Dorado, Reserve $13.00	S	S		B	B				
LOUIS M. MARTINI WINERY '91, Napa Vly. $8.00	B	S					B	B	
MC ILROY WINES '91, Russian River, Aquarious $14.50		S				S	S	S	
MIRASSOU VINEYARDS '91, Monterey, Family Selection $9.75	B		B			S		B	

L.A.	Orange Farmers	San Fran	Dallas	State Fair	New World	W. Coast	San Diego	Chardonnay
				4 AWARDS				
S		S		G	B			**NAPA RIDGE** '91, North Coast, Reserve $12.00
		B	B		B		B	**NAVARRO VINEYARDS** '91, Mendocino $11.00
S	B	S	B					**R. H. PHILLIP VINEYARD** '92, California, Barrel Cuvee $8.00
B	B	B			B			**QUAIL RIDGE CELLARS** '90, Napa Vly. $15.00
		S	S			S	B	**RAYMOND VINEYARD** '91, Napa Vly., Reserve $17.00
S		G	S				S	**ROMBAUER VINEYARDS** '91, Carneros $15.00
	B	S	B		S			**SWANSON VINEYARDS** '90, Napa Vly., Estate $16.00
	G	S	B		B			**TAFT STREET WINERY** '91, Sonoma Co. $8.00
S		S			B	B		**TROUT GULCH VINEYARDS** '90, Santa Cruz Mtns. $14.00
G	Σ	S			S			**VILLA MT. EDEN WINERY** '91, California, Cellar Select $10.00
B		B	G		S			**WINDSOR VINEYARDS** '91, Sonoma, Signature Series $20.00
	B	B			B	S		**ZD WINES** '91, California $20.50
				3 AWARDS				
B	B			S				**S. ANDERSON VINEYARD** '91, Stag's Leap Dist., Estate $18.00
		B		B	B			**ARCIERO WINERY** '91, Paso Robles, Estate $7.59
S		B		S				**ARMIDA WINERY** '91, Russian River Vly. $10.00
G	B	S						**BAILEYANA** '91, Edna Vly., Paragon Vnyds.
B	B	S						**BARON HERZOG WINE CELLARS** '91, California $10.75
		B	B		B			**BEAUCANON** '91, Napa Vly., LH $10.00

Chardonnay

	L.A.	Orange Farmers	San Fran	Dallas	State Fair	New World	W. Coast	San Diego
3 AWARDS								
BELVEDERE WINERY '90, Russian River Vly. $13.00		S	G			B		
BYRON VINEYARD '91, Santa Barbara Co. $14.00		S			G	Σ		
MAURICE CARRIE WINERY '91, Temecula Vly., Reserve $9.00		B	G				S	
CHALK HILL WINERY '91, Sonoma Co., Chalk Hill $17.00	G				G	Σ		
CHATEAU DE LEU WINERY '90, Napa Vly. $11.00		B					S	S
CHATEAU SOUVERAIN '91, Sonoma Co., Barrel Ferm. $10.00	G				S	G		
CHAUFEE-EAU CELLARS '91, Carneros, Sangiacomo $16.00			B		S			S
CINNABAR '90, Santa Cruz Mtns. $20.00			S				B	G
CLOS DU BOIS '91, Alexander Vly.					B	B	G	
CLOS DU VAL '91, Napa Vly., Carneros $14.00		B	S			B		
CLOS PEGASE WINERY '90, Napa Vly. $13.00		S				B	B	
DE LOACH VINEYARDS '91, Russian River Vly. $15.00		B	S		B			
FETZER VINEYARDS '92, California, Sundial $8.00	S	S				B		
GAINEY VINEYARD '91, Santa Barbara Co. $13.00	G				S	B		
GEYSER PEAK WINERY '91, Alexander Vly., Reserve $15.00		B	B	B				
GUGLIELMO WINERY '92, Monterey Co., Mt. Madonna $8.25	B	B	S					
HAHN ESTATES '91, Monterey $9.00	G	S	B					
HANDLEY CELLARS '90, Dry Creek Vly. $14.50					B	B	B	
HAWK CREST '92, California $9.00			B		B			B

3 AWARDS

L.A.	Orange Farmers	San Fran	Dallas	State Fair	New World	W. Coast	San Diego	
B		B			S			**HIDDEN CELLARS** '91, Mendocino Co., Reserve $16.00
		S	S		B			**KENDALL-JACKSON WINERY** '92, California, Vintner's Reserve $13.00
		B	B		S			**KONRAD ESTATE** '91, Mendocino Co. $12.00
	S	B					S	**LOCKWOOD VINEYARD** '91, Monterey $8.00
B					G	B		**MACROSTIE WINERY** '91, Carneros $14.75
		S		Σ	S			**MIRASSOU VINEYARDS** '91, Monterey, Harvest Reserve $12.50
		B	B		S			**MURPHY-GOODE WINERY** '91, Alexander Vly., Estate $12.50
				B	B	G		**NEWLAN VINEYARDS** '91, Napa Vly. $14.00
B					B			**OBESTER WINERY** '90, Mendocino Co., Barrel Ferm.
B		B			B			**JOSEPH PHELPS VINEYARDS** '91, Napa Vly.
		S	S					**PINNACLES ESTATE** '91, Monterey Co.
S		B			B			**RABBIT RIDGE VINEYARDS** '91, Russian River Vly. $16.00
		B			S			**RAYMOND VINEYARD** '90, Napa Vly. $13.00
G		B	S					**ROCHIOLI VINEYARD** '91, Russian River $15.00
B		S	B					**ROUND HILL CELLARS** '91, Napa Vly., Reserve $11.00
		S			S			**SANTA BARBARA WINERY** '90, Santa Barbara Co., Reserve $20.00
G		Σ			S			**SEBASTIANI VINEYARDS** '91, Sonoma Co., Reserve
		G			B	S		**SEBASTIANI VINEYARDS** '91, Sonoma Series $9.00
B	S				B			**SHAFER VINEYARDS** '91, Napa Vly., Barrel Select $15.00

Chardonnay

	L.A.	Orange Farmers	San Fran	Dallas	State Fair	New World	W. Coast	San Diego
3 AWARDS								
ST. FRANCIS WINERY '91, Sonoma Vly., Reserve $15.00			G	S	B			
ST. SUPERY WINERY '91, Napa Vly., Dollarhide Ranch $12.50	S	G				B		
STORRS WINERY '91, Santa Cruz Mtns.	S				B			B
SUTTER HOME '91, California $5.95		B			B	G		
VICHON WINERY '91, Napa Vly. $15.00		B			B			S
VILLA MT. EDEN WINERY '91, Carneros, Grand Reserve $15.00	B				S	S		
WHITE OAK VINEYARDS '91, Sonoma Co. $12.95					B	B	B	
WILD HORSE WINERY '92, Central Coast $14.00		G		B	B			
ZACA MESA WINERY '90, Santa Barbara Co., Reserve $16.50	S				B	B		
2 AWARDS								
ACACIA '91, Napa, Carneros			Σ		B			
ALDERBROOK WINERY '90, Dry Creek Vly. $11.00			S					B
WILLIAM BACCALA ESTATE '91, Sonoma $10.00				B	B			
BAREFOOT CELLARS 'NV, California $4.00		B						B
BEAULIEU VINEYARD '91, Napa Vly., Beautour $7.85	S				B			
BEAULIEU VINEYARD '90, Napa Vly., Carneros Reserve $17.00					B			S
BELVEDERE WINERY '91, Alexander Vly. $9.00		B		B				
BELVEDERE WINERY '90, Sonoma Co. $18.00		S						S
BENZIGER WINERY '91, Carneros $16.00			G		S			
BERGFELD WINERY '91, Napa Vly., Estate $11.00		S						B

2 AWARDS

L.A.	Orange	Farmers	San Fran	Dallas	State Fair	New World	W. Coast	San Diego	
			S					S	**BERINGER VINEYARDS** '91, Napa Vly., Sbragia
			B			S			**DAVID BRUCE WINERY** '91, Santa Cruz, Meyley Vnyd. $18.00
G	B								**DAVID BRUCE WINERY** '90, Santa Cruz Mtns., Reserve $30.00
	G					B			**CALE CELLARS** '91, Carneros, Sangiacomo Vnyd. $18.00
S						B			**CHATEAU JULIEN WINERY** '91, Monterey Co., Surlie, Reserve $13.00
	B		B						**COOK'S CHAMPAGNE CELLARS** '91, California, Reserve
	B		B						**CORBETT CANYON VINEYARDS** '91, Central Coast, Coastal Classic $8.00
			B			S			**COSENTINO WINERY** '91, Napa Vly. $14.00
B						S			**DOMAINE DE CLARCK** '91, Monterey Co. $14.00
			B			S			**DOMAINE ST. GEORGE WINERY** '92, California, Reserve $8.50
			G			Σ			**DREYER SONOMA WINERY** '91, Sonoma Co., Carneros $15.00
				B		B			**EDMEADES** '91, Mendocino $16.00
	B					B			**GARY FARRELL WINES** '91, Russian River Vly., Allen Vnyd. $18.00
			B			S			**FENESTRA WINERY** '91, Livermore Vly., Toy Vnyd. $12.50
						B	G		**FREEMARK ABBEY** '90, Napa Vly. $15.00
			B	B					**GABRIELLI WINERY** '91, Mendocino Co. $16.00
						S	G		**GUENOC WINERY** '92, North Coast $11.00
B			B						**GUENOC WINERY** '91, Guenoc Vly., Estate $14.00
	B					S			**GUENOC WINERY** '90, Genevieve Magoon Res. $22.00

Chardonnay	L.A.	Orange Farmers	San Fran	Dallas	State Fair	New World	W. Coast	San Diego
2 AWARDS								
HOP KILN WINERY '91, Russian River, Griffin Vnyds. $15.00					B	B		
HUSCH VINEYARDS '91, Mendocino, Estate $11.00	S	S						
INDIAN SPRINGS VINEYARDS '91, Sierra Foothills, Reserve $16.00		S	B					
JEKEL VINEYARDS '89, Arroyo Seco, Sanctuary, Sceptre	B				S			
ROBERT KEENAN WINERY '91, Napa Vly.	B				B			
KENDALL-JACKSON WINERY '91, Santa Maria, Camelot Vnyd. $14.00		S				S		
KENWOOD VINEYARDS '91, Sonoma Vly., Reserve	G				B			
LANDMARK VINEYARDS '91, Sonoma, Two Williams Vnyd. $14.00		B			G			
LANDMARK VINEYARDS '90, Alex. Vly., Damaris Reserve $16.00				S		B		
LEEWARD WINERY '90, Monterey $14.00			B			G		
LOCKWOOD VINEYARD '91, Monterey, Estate, Reserve $14.00		S						G
LOLONIS WINERY '91, Mendocino Co., Reserve $19.00		S			G			
LYNFRED WINERY '90, California Reserve, Barrel Ferm.	B							S
MERRYVALE VINEYARDS '91, Napa Vly., Starmont $16.00			S		B			
MIRASSOU VINEYARDS '90, Monterey, Harvest Reserve $12.50					S	S		
MORGAN '91, Monterey, Reserve $23.00				S	B			
MOUNT VEEDER WINERY '91, Napa Vly. $17.00		S						B
NAPA RIDGE '92, Central Coast, Coastal Vines	B				B			
NAVARRO VINEYARDS '90, Mendocino $11.00			G			G		

L.A.	Orange Farmers	San Fran	Dallas	State Fair	New World	W. Coast	San Diego	Chardonnay
					2 AWARDS			
	G				B			**NAVARRO VINEYARDS** '89, Anderson Vly., Reserve $16.00
		B				S		**OLIVET LANE ESTATE** '91, Russian River Vly. $11.00
		S	B					**PARAISO SPRINGS VINEYARDS** '91, Monterey
		B				S		**J. PEDRONCELLI WINERY** '91, Dry Creek Vly. $9.00
				S	B			**PENARD** '91, Carneros $19.00
						S	G	**RANCHO SISQUOC** '91, Santa Maria Vly., Estate $14.00
B					B			**ROMBAUER VINEYARDS** '90, Napa Vly., Reserve $20.00
B	B							**ROYCE VINEYARDS** '91, California
		B				S		**RUTHERFORD ESTATE CELLARS** '91, Napa Vly. $7.00
					S	B		**RUTHERFORD HILL WINERY** '90, Napa Vly., Jaeger Vnyds. $12.00
		B					B	**SEQUOIA GROVE VINEYARDS** '91, Napa Vly., Carneros $14.00
		B	B					**SIMI WINERY** '91, Sonoma/Mendocino/Napa $12.00
S	S							**SIMI WINERY** '90, Mendocino/Sonoma/Napa $12.00
B					B			**SONOMA CREEK WINERY** '91, Carneros, Barrel Ferm. $11.00
	B				B			**ST. CLEMENT VINEYARDS** '91, Napa Vly. $16.00
B		B						**STAG'S LEAP WINE CELLARS** '91, Napa Vly. $18.00
					B	B		**STERLING VINEYARDS** '89, Napa, Diamond Mt. Ranch $18.00
	B	B						**STONE CREEK CELLARS** '91, California
		B			B			**STONY RIDGE WINERY** '91, California Collection $6.50

Chardonnay	L.A.	Orange Farmers	San Fran	Dallas	State Fair	New World	W. Coast	San Diego
2 AWARDS								
STORRS WINERY '91, Santa Cruz Mtns., Meyley Vnyd. $18.00		S		B				
RODNEY STRONG VINEYARDS '92, Sonoma Co. $9.00		B		B				
SUNRISE '91, Livermore Vly., Beyers Ranch $10.00		S			G			
SWANSON VINEYARDS '90, Napa Vly, Estate Reserve $20.00			G					B
TRENTADUE '91, Alexander Vly. $9.00				B				B
VENTANA VINEYARDS '90, Monterey, Gold Stripe Sel. $10.00	S							B
VENTANA VINEYARDS '90, Monterey, Crystal, Barrel Ferm.						B		B
VENTANA VINEYARDS '89, Monterey, Eagle, Estate $16.00		G			Σ			
VICHON WINERY '91, California, Coastal Selection $9.00		B					B	
WENTE BROS. '91, Livermore Vly., Estate Reserve $16.00		B	B					
WENTE BROS. '91, Arroyo Seco, Riva Ranch Vnyd. $14.00		B				B		
WHITFORD CELLARS '90, Napa Vly., Haynes Vnyd.	B							B
WILDHURST VINEYARDS '91, Sonoma Co. $11.00		B		B				
WINDSOR VINEYARDS '91, Russian River Vly., Reserve $14.00				B				B
WINDSOR VINEYARDS '91, Russian River, Preston Ranch					B	B		
WOODSIDE VINEYARDS '91, Santa Cruz Mtns., Estate $16.00				S				S
ZACA MESA WINERY '91, Santa Barbara Co. $11.00					B			S

Baron Herzog

CALIFORNIA
CHENIN BLANC

1992

PRODUCED AND BOTTLED BY BARON HERZOG WINE CELLARS, CO.
SAN MARTIN, CALIFORNIA, U.S.A. • ALC. 12% BY VOL. ⓊP

ESTATE BOTTLED
HUSCH
LA RIBERA VINEYARDS

1992
MENDOCINO
CHENIN BLANC

GROWN, PRODUCED AND BOTTLED BY THE H.A. OSWALD FAMILY
PHILO, CA. ALCOHOL 12.2% BY VOLUME, RESIDUAL SUGAR 1.8%

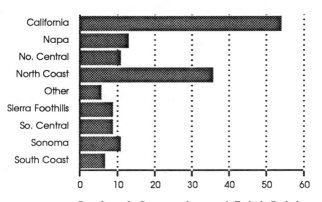

Chenin Blanc

Regional Comparison of Total Points

(Gold-plus=7 Gold=5 Silver=3 Bronze=1)

Highest individual wine totals

15 BARON HERZOG WINE CELLARS
  '92, California $5.95

12 HUSCH VINEYARDS
  '92, Mendocino, La Ribera Vnyd. $7.50

11 DRY CREEK VINEYARD
  '92, California $7.00

11 SIMI WINERY
  '91, Mendocino Co. $7.00

10 PARDUCCI WINE CELLARS
  '92, Mendocino Co. $6.00

7 MAURICE CARRIE WINERY
  '91, Temecula, Soft $4.00

6 NAPA RIDGE
  '91, Central Coast $5.75

6 R. H. PHILLIP VINEYARD
  '91, California $5.00

6 PRESTON VINEYARDS
  '91, Dry Creek Vly., Estate $7.00

Chenin Blanc

	L.A.	Orange Farmers	San Fran	Dallas	State Fair	New World	W. Coast	San Diego
5 AWARDS								
BARON HERZOG WINE CELLARS '92, California $5.95	B	S			B	Σ		S
DRY CREEK VINEYARD '92, California $7.00		B	B		S		B	G
4 AWARDS								
HUSCH VINEYARDS '92, Mendocino, La Ribera Vnyd. $7.50		G			G		B	B
PARDUCCI WINE CELLARS '92, Mendocino Co. $6.00	S	G			B	B		
3 AWARDS								
MAURICE CARRIE WINERY '91, Temecula, Soft $4.00	B	G					B	
GREENSTONE '92, Amador Co. $5.00	B	S			B			
CHARLES KRUG WINERY '92, Napa Vly. $6.50			B	B			B	
R. H. PHILLIP VINEYARD '92, California $5.00		S			B		B	
SIMI WINERY '91, Mendocino Co. $7.00			S	S	G			
WINDSOR VINEYARDS '92, Alexander Vly. $7.00		S			B		B	
2 AWARDS								
BERINGER VINEYARDS '92, Napa Vly., Beringer Vnyds. $7.50		B			B			
DRY CREEK VINEYARD '91, California $7.00					B	S		
GRAND CRU VINEYARDS '92, California, Premium Selection $6.50		B	B					
HUSCH VINEYARDS '91, Mendocino, La Ribera Vnyd. $7.50					B	B		
MIRASSOU VINEYARDS '91, Monterey $6.50					B		S	
NAPA RIDGE '91, Central Coast $5.75		S				S		
R. H. PHILLIP VINEYARD '91, California $5.00					S	S		
PRESTON VINEYARDS '91, Dry Creek Vly., Estate $7.00		G			B			

L.A. Orange Farmers	San Fran Dallas State Fair	New World W. Coast San Diego	Chenin Blanc
		2 *AWARDS*	
B		S	**SANTA BARBARA WINERY** '90, Santa Ynez Vly. Barrel Ferm. $8.00

FETZER

1 9 9 2

GEWÜRZTRAMINER

C A L I F O R N I A

ALCOHOL 10.9% BY VOLUME

1992

LAWRENCE J. BARGETTO

MONTEREY COUNTY

Gewurztraminer

PRODUCED AND BOTTLED BY BARGETTO WINERY, SOQUEL, CALIFORNIA, USA ALC. 11.5% BY VOL.

Gewurztraminer

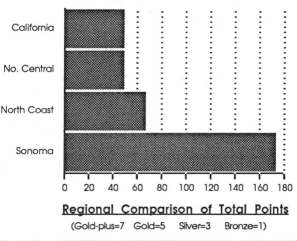

Regional Comparison of Total Points

(Gold-plus=7 Gold=5 Silver=3 Bronze=1)

Highest individual wine totals

36 **FETZER VINEYARDS**
'92, California $7.00

26 **BARGETTO WINERY**
'92, Monterey Co. $8.00

20 **NAVARRO VINEYARDS**
'91, North Coast, LH $12.00

DE LOACH VINEYARDS
'92, Russian River., Early Harvest $8.50

18 **GEYSER PEAK WINERY**
'92, Sonoma Co. $5.50

18 **GAN EDEN**
'92, Russian River Vly., LH $8.00

18 **DE LOACH VINEYARDS**
'91, Russian River Vly., LH $14.00

16 **WINDSOR VINEYARDS**
'92, Alexander Vly. $7.00

16 **THOMAS FOGARTY WINERY**
'92, Monterey, Ventana Vnyd. $11.50

14 **HANDLEY CELLARS**
'92, Anderson Vly. $8.00

Gewurztraminer 0 – 3.0 Residual Sugar	L.A.	Orange	Farmers	San Fran	Dallas	State Fair	New World	W. Coast	San Diego
8 AWARDS									
GEYSER PEAK WINERY '92, Sonoma Co. $5.50		B	B	B	G	G	B	S	B
6 AWARDS									
ADLER FELS WINERY '92, Sonoma Co. $9.00			S	B	S	S		S	Σ
BARGETTO WINERY '92, Monterey Co. $8.00	S	G	Σ			B		G	G
HANDLEY CELLARS '92, Anderson Vly. $8.00	G	B		S		B		B	S
WINDSOR VINEYARDS '92, Alexander Vly. $7.00	S	B		B		S	G		S
5 AWARDS									
DE LOACH VINEYARDS '92, Russian River., Early Harvest $8.50	S		Σ	S		S			S
HOP KILN WINERY '92, Russian River, Griffin Vnyds. $7.50		G	S	B				S	B
HUSCH VINEYARDS '91, Anderson Vly. $8.50			S		B	B		B	B
NAVARRO VINEYARDS '91, Anderson Vly., Cuvee $8.50		S	S	B		B	G		
4 AWARDS									
DAVIS BYNUM WINERY '92, Russian River Vly. $8.00			S				B	S	B
THOMAS FOGARTY WINERY '92, Monterey, Ventana Vnyd. $11.50			Σ	S		B			G
3 AWARDS									
ALDERBROOK WINERY '92, Russian River Vly. $8.00	S		B	S					
GUNDLACH-BUNDSCHU '92, Sonoma Vly., Rhinefarm $8.00	B	S		S					
PARDUCCI WINE CELLARS '92, Mendocino Co. $7.25	G	G				B			
STORRS WINERY '92, Monterey Viento Vnyd. $9.00	S	S				B			
2 AWARDS									
BERINGER VINEYARDS '92, California, Prop. Grown $7.50		S				B			

Gewurztraminer
0 - 3.0 Residual Sugar

L.A.	Orange	Farmers	San Fran	Dallas	State Fair	New World	W. Coast	San Diego	
									2 AWARDS
			B			S			**DE LOACH VINEYARDS** '91, Russian River, Early Harvest $8.50
			B			S			**FIRESTONE VINEYARD** '92, California $9.00
B	B								**MILL CREEK VINEYARDS** '92, Dry Creek Vly., Estate
				S		S			**MOSBY** '91, Santa Barbara, Barrel Ferm. $8.00

Gewurztraminer
3.1+ Residual Sugar

L.A.	Orange	Farmers	San Fran	Dallas	State Fair	New World	W. Coast	San Diego	
									8 AWARDS
S	B	G	G	B		Σ	Σ	Σ	**FETZER VINEYARDS** '92, California, R.S. 3.5 $7.00
									6 AWARDS
		G	B		B	B	Σ	S	**GAN EDEN** '92, Russian River Vly., LH, R.S. 6.0 $8.00
		S	S		S	S	G	S	**NAVARRO VINEYARDS** '91, North Coast, LH, R.S. 7.9 $12.00
									4 AWARDS
					S	G	G	G	**DE LOACH VINEYARDS** '91, Russian River Vly., LH, R.S. 13.5 $14.00
									3 AWARDS
	B					S			**CHATEAU ST. JEAN** '91, Frank Johnson, SLH, R.S. 10.6 $15.00
									2 AWARDS
			B	B					**DE LOACH VINEYARDS** '92, Russian River Vly., LH, R.S. 13.5 $14.00
			B			B			**NAPA RIDGE** '91, Central Coast, R.S. 3.1 $7.50

1992

GEYSER PEAK

SOFT JOHANNISBERG RIESLING

NORTH COAST

ALC. 9.8% BY VOL.

Johannisberg Riesling

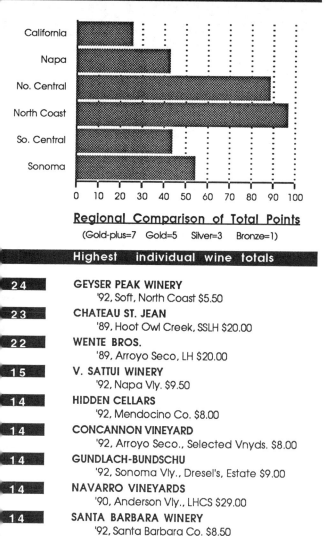

Regional Comparison of Total Points

(Gold-plus=7   Gold=5   Silver=3   Bronze=1)

Highest individual wine totals

24   **GEYSER PEAK WINERY**
'92, Soft, North Coast $5.50

23   **CHATEAU ST. JEAN**
'89, Hoot Owl Creek, SSLH $20.00

22   **WENTE BROS.**
'89, Arroyo Seco, LH $20.00

15   **V. SATTUI WINERY**
'92, Napa Vly. $9.50

14   **HIDDEN CELLARS**
'92, Mendocino Co. $8.00

14   **CONCANNON VINEYARD**
'92, Arroyo Seco., Selected Vnyds. $8.00

14   **GUNDLACH-BUNDSCHU**
'92, Sonoma Vly., Dresel's, Estate $9.00

14   **NAVARRO VINEYARDS**
'90, Anderson Vly., LHCS $29.00

14   **SANTA BARBARA WINERY**
'92, Santa Barbara Co. $8.50

13   **J. LOHR WINERY**
'92, Monterey, "Bay Mist" $7.25

13   **V. SATTUI WINERY**
'92, Napa Vly., Off Dry $10.00

13   **WINDSOR VINEYARDS**
'92, Russian River Vly., LeBaron Vnyd. $7.50

Johannisberg Riesling
0 – 3.0 Residual Sugar

	L.A.	Orange Farmers	San Fran	Dallas	State Fair	New World	W. Coast	San Diego
8 AWARDS								
GEYSER PEAK WINERY — '92, Soft, North Coast $5.50	S	G	G	S	B	B	G	B
7 AWARDS								
V. SATTUI WINERY — '92, Napa Vly. $9.50	S	S	B		B	B	S	S
5 AWARDS								
J. LOHR WINERY — '92, Monterey, "Bay Mist" $7.25	B	G	S		B	S		
V. SATTUI WINERY — '92, Napa Vly., Off Dry $10.00	B		S		S	B	G	
WINDSOR VINEYARDS — '92, Russian River Vly., LeBaron Vnyd. $7.50	S	B	S		B		G	
4 AWARDS								
CONCANNON VINEYARD — '92, Arroyo Seco., Selected Vnyds. $8.00	G		Σ		B			B
FETZER VINEYARDS — '92, California $7.00	B		B		G	G		
GREENWOOD RIDGE VINEYARDS — '92, Anderson Vly., White $8.50		B	S		B			B
GUNDLACH-BUNDSCHU — '92, Sonoma Vly., Dresel's, Estate $9.00			S		S		S	G
HARMONY CELLARS — '92, Paso Robles $8.00	S				G	B	S	
KONOCTI WINERY — '92, Lake Co. $7.50		B	S				S	B
SANTA BARBARA WINERY — '92, Santa Barbara Co. $8.50			S		S		G	S
3 AWARDS								
BERINGER VINEYARDS — '91, North Coast $8.00			S		B			B
MADDALENA VINEYARD — '92, Central Coast $5.00		B	B					
NAVARRO VINEYARDS — '91, Anderson Vly. $8.50		G	S				S	
2 AWARDS								
BERINGER VINEYARDS — '92, California, Beringer Vnyds. $7.50		B			B			

2 AWARDS

L.A.	Orange Farmers	San Fran	Dallas	State Fair	New World	W. Coast	San Diego	
		B			B			**CALLAWAY VINEYARD** '92, Temecula $7.00
		S	B					**FETZER VINEYARDS** '91, California $7.00
		B	G					**FIRESTONE VINEYARD** '91, Santa Ynez Vly. $7.50
B	B							**KENDALL-JACKSON WINERY** '92, California, Vintner's Reserve
		G	G					**J. LOHR WINERY** '91, Monterey, "Bay Mist" $7.00
			S	S				**NAVARRO VINEYARDS** '92, Anderson Vly. $9.00
B	B							**RENAISSANCE VINEYARD** '91, North Yuba, Estate $8.00
S					S			**RIVER RUN** '92, Monterey Co. $7.00
		S			B			**STONY RIDGE WINERY** '92, Monterey Co., Ltd. Release $5.50
				B	S			**VENTANA VINEYARDS** '91, Monterey, Estate $6.00

Johannisberg Riesling
3.1+ Residual Sugar

	L.A.	Orange Farmers	San Fran	Dallas	State Fair	New World	W. Coast	San Diego
6 AWARDS								
HIDDEN CELLARS '92, Mendocino Co., R.S. 4.5 $8.00	G	S	S		B		B	B
WENTE BROS. '89, Arroyo Seco, LH, R.S. 13.3 $20.00		G	S	Σ	S	B		S
5 AWARDS								
CHATEAU ST. JEAN '89, Hoot Owl Creek, SSLH, R.S. 24.9 $20.00	Σ				G	S	G	S
4 AWARDS								
NAVARRO VINEYARDS '90, Anderson Vly., LHCS, R.S. 19.2 $29.00	B	Σ	G			B		
2 AWARDS								
CONCANNON VINEYARD '92, Anderson Vly., LH, $8.95			B					B
FREEMARK ABBEY '91, Napa, Edelwein Gold, R.S. 21.0 $25.00			B		B			
GRAND CRU VINEYARDS '91, California, R.S. 4.5 $6.50			B	B				
NEWLAN VINEYARDS '91, Napa Vly., LH	B				S			
SANTINO WINES '89, Sonoma Co., DBSH, R.S. 27.7 $18.00			B		B			

BENZIGER

1990

SONOMA COUNTY

MERLOT

ALCOHOL 12.8% BY VOLUME

VILLA
MT. EDEN

Grand 1990 *Reserve*
MERLOT
NAPA VALLEY

Merlot

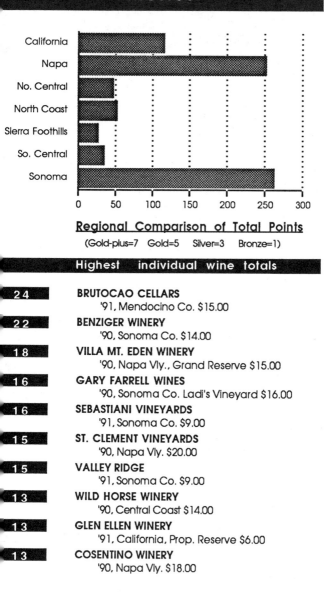

California
Napa
No. Central
North Coast
Sierra Foothills
So. Central
Sonoma

0   50   100   150   200   250   300

Regional Comparison of Total Points

(Gold-plus=7   Gold=5   Silver=3   Bronze=1)

Highest individual wine totals

24 **BRUTOCAO CELLARS**
'91, Mendocino Co. $15.00

22 **BENZIGER WINERY**
'90, Sonoma Co. $14.00

18 **VILLA MT. EDEN WINERY**
'90, Napa Vly., Grand Reserve $15.00

16 **GARY FARRELL WINES**
'90, Sonoma Co. Ladi's Vineyard $16.00

16 **SEBASTIANI VINEYARDS**
'91, Sonoma Co. $9.00

15 **ST. CLEMENT VINEYARDS**
'90, Napa Vly. $20.00

15 **VALLEY RIDGE**
'91, Sonoma Co. $9.00

13 **WILD HORSE WINERY**
'90, Central Coast $14.00

13 **GLEN ELLEN WINERY**
'91, California, Prop. Reserve $6.00

13 **COSENTINO WINERY**
'90, Napa Vly. $18.00

Merlot

	L.A.	Orange Farmers	San Fran	Dallas	State Fair	New World	W. Coast	San Diego
8 AWARDS								
BRUTOCAO CELLARS '91, Mendocino Co. $15.00	B	G	B	B	S	G	Σ	B
6 AWARDS								
BENZIGER WINERY '90, Sonoma Co. $14.00	S	S	S		G		S	G
VILLA MT. EDEN WINERY '90, Napa Vly., Grand Reserve $15.00	G		S	S	B	S		S
5 AWARDS								
MAURICE CARRIE WINERY '91, California $8.00			S	B		S	B	S
CHATEAU SOUVERAIN '90, Alexander Vly. $10.50			B		B	S	B	B
GEYSER PEAK WINERY '91, Alexander Vly. $12.00			G	B	B	S	B	
GLEN ELLEN WINERY '91, California, Prop. Reserve $6.00			G	S	B	B	S	
GOLDEN CREEK VINEYARD '90, Sonoma Co. $12.00			S	B	B	B	S	
ST. CLEMENT VINEYARDS '90, Napa Vly. $20.00			B	S	G	G	B	
VALLEY RIDGE '91, Sonoma Co. $9.00			B	S	S	G	S	
WENTE BROS. '90, Livermore Vly., Crane Ridge $14.00	B	B		S	B		S	
4 AWARDS								
BEL ARBORS '91, California, Founder's Sel $7.00			G		B	B		S
CHESTNUT HILL '91, North Coast, Coastal Cuvee $10.50			Σ		B	B		
CLOS DU BOIS '90, Sonoma Co. $15.00			B			S	S	
COOK'S CHAMPAGNE CELLARS '91, California, Captain's Reserve $6.00				B		B	S	
CORBETT CANYON VINEYARDS '91, California Coastal Classic $7.00			B	S				Σ
GARY FARRELL WINES '90, Sonoma Co. Ladi's Vineyard $16.00			G	B	S			
FETZER VINEYARDS '90, California Eagle Peak $8.00			B	B			S	

L.A.	Orange Farmers	San Fran	Dallas	State Fair	New World	W. Coast	San Diego	Merlot
					4 AWARDS			
B		S			B	S		**ROBERT KEENAN WINERY** '90, Napa Vly. $18.00
B	G	S			S			**MILL CREEK VINEYARDS** '89, Dry Creek, Estate $12.00
S	Σ			B	G			**SEBASTIANI VINEYARDS** '91, Sonoma Co. $9.00
S		S		S	S			**SHAFER VINEYARDS** '91, Napa Vly. $20.00
B	S	S	B					**ST. SUPERY WINERY** '90, Napa Vly., Dollarhide Ranch
B		S			B	S		**STONY RIDGE WINERY** '91, North Coast, Ltd. Release $9.00
					3 AWARDS			
B	B				B			**ARMIDA WINERY** '90, Russian River Vly. $12.00
		S			S	S		**BELVEDERE WINERY** '90, Dry Creek Vly. $14.00
B	B	B						**BERGFELD WINERY** '89, Napa Vly., Estate
		S	B		B			**BOGLE VINEYARDS** '91, California $8.00
		S		G	B			**CHATEAU SOUVERAIN** '91, Alexander Vly. $10.50
B		S	B					**CHATEAU ST. JEAN** '89, Sonoma Co. $17.00
S	B	B						**CONN CREEK WINERY** '89, Napa Vly., Barrel Select
B	Σ			G				**COSENTINO WINERY** '90, Napa Vly. $18.00
	G	B			B			**CRESTON VINEYARDS** '90, Paso Robles $13.00
		S	B		S			**CYPRESS** '91, California $9.00
G	S		B					**DRY CREEK VINEYARD** '90, Dry Creek Vly. $14.00
		B	B		G			**FETZER VINEYARDS** '91, California, Eagle Peak $8.00

Merlot

	L.A.	Orange	Farmers	San Fran	Dallas	State Fair	New World	W. Coast	San Diego
3 AWARDS									
FLORA SPRINGS '91, Napa, Floreal $12.00	S			B	B				
FRANCISCAN OAKVILLE ESTATE '90, Napa Vly. $14.50				S			G		B
GOLD HILL VINEYARD '90, El Dorado Co. $11.00				B	B	S			
JANKRIS VINEYARD '91, Paso Robles $9.00				B		B			Σ
JEKEL VINEYARDS '90, Monterey $10.95	G	S				S			
KENDALL-JACKSON WINERY '91, California, Vintner's Reserve $14.00	B	S				S			
KENDALL-JACKSON WINERY '90, California Vintner's Reserve $14.00		G					S		B
CHARLES KRUG WINERY '90, Napa Vly., Estate $13.25	B	S		B					
LAVA CAP WINERY '90, El Dorado Co., Estate $13.00	B							S	B
MIRASSOU VINEYARDS '91, Monterey Co., Family Sel. $9.00	B				B		B		
NEVADA CITY WINERY '90, Sierra Foothills $14.00	G	B					G		
ROYCE VINEYARDS '91, Sonoma Co.						B	G		Σ
SEBASTIANI VINEYARDS '90, Sonoma Co.					B	S	Σ		
STONE CREEK CELLARS '91, California, Special Selection $6.25	B						B	S	
WILD HORSE WINERY '90, Central Coast $14.00	G						Σ	B	
WILDHURST VINEYARDS '91, Clear Lake $11.00	S				G			B	
J. WILE & SONS '90, Napa Vly. $7.00	B				B				B
2 AWARDS									
BERGFELD WINERY '90, Napa Vly.							S	B	
BERINGER VINEYARDS '89, Howell Mtn., Bancroft Ranch $28.50	S						S		

Merlot

2 AWARDS

L.A.	Orange Farmers	San Fran	Dallas	State Fair	New World	W. Coast	San Diego	
		B	B					**DAVIS BYNUM WINERY** '91, Sonoma Co., Ltd. Release $13.00
					B	G			**CLOS PEGASE WINERY** '90, Napa Vly. $15.50
S		S						**DOMAINE ST. GEORGE WINERY** '89, Chalk Hill, Premiere Cuvee $8.00
	B						S	**DUNNEWOOD** '90, California, Barrel Select $6.00
					B			**FENESTRA WINERY** '90, Livermore Vly. $13.00
G	B							**FIRESTONE VINEYARD** '91, Santa Ynez Vly. $12.00
	B	S						**GAINEY VINEYARD** '90, Santa Ynez Vly.
	B				B			**GARLAND RANCH** '91, California $7.00
						G		**GUGLIELMO WINERY** '91, Napa Vly., Mt. Madonna
		S			B			**GUNDLACH-BUNDSCHU** '90, Sonoma, Rhinefarm Vnyds. $16.00
B		S						**INDIAN SPRINGS VINEYARDS** '91, Nevada Co. $12.00
				S	B			**TOBIN JAMES** '91, Paso Robles, Full Moon $14.00
	B				B			**KAUTZ IRONSTONE** '90, California, "Highlands" $10.00
S					B			**KENWOOD VINEYARDS** '90, Sonoma Co. $15.00
				G	G			**LOCKWOOD VINEYARD** '91, Monterey $9.00
		B						**M. MARION** '91, Napa Vly.
					B			**MARKHAM VINEYARDS** '90, Napa Vly. $15.00
G					B			**PAUL MASSON VINEYARDS** '91, Monterey Co. $8.00
		B			S			**MONTEREY PENINSULA WINERY** '87, Monterey, Dr's Reserve

57

Merlot	L.A.	Orange	Farmers	San Fran	Dallas	State Fair	New World	W. Coast	San Diego
2 AWARDS									
JOSEPH PHELPS VINEYARDS '90, Napa Vly. $16.00	G				B				
QUAIL RIDGE CELLARS '89, Napa Vly. $15.00					B		B		
RAVENSWOOD '90, Sonoma Co. $15.00	G				G				
RICHARDSON VINEYARDS '91, Sangiacomo/Gregory Vnyds. $15.00	G							B	
ROUND HILL CELLARS '90, Napa Vly., Reserve $11.00							G		B
RUTHERFORD HILL WINERY '89, Napa Vly. $14.00	S								B
SALAMANDRE WINE CELLARS '91, Arroyo Seco $14.00	S			B					
SILVERADO VINEYARDS '90, Stag's Leap Dist. $16.50	B								S
ST. FRANCIS WINERY '90, Sonoma Vly. $17.00						B	G		
SWANSON VINEYARDS '90, Napa Vly., Estate $15.00	S						S		
TRUCHARD VINEYARDS '90, Napa Vly.						B	S		
M. G. VALLEJO WINERY '91, California Harvest Select $7.50	B	B							
VENDANGE '91, California $6.00	B			S					
WINDSOR VINEYARDS '90, Russian River Vly.								G	S

CHRISTOPHER CREEK

ESTATE BOTTLED

1990

RUSSIAN RIVER VALLEY

PETITE SIRAH

SONOMA COUNTY

ALCOHOL 13% BY VOL.

VINTAGE 1991

GRANITE SPRINGS

EL DORADO

Petite Sirah

PRODUCED & BOTTLED BY GRANITE SPRINGS WINERY
SOMERSET, CALIFORNIA ALCOHOL 13% BY VOLUME

Petite Sirah

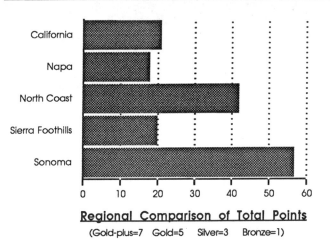

Regional Comparison of Total Points
(Gold-plus=7 Gold=5 Silver=3 Bronze=1)

Highest individual wine totals

18 **CHRISTOPHER CREEK**
'90, Russian River Vly. $13.00

12 **RABBIT RIDGE VINEYARDS**
'90, Sonoma Co. $9.50

11 **DAVID BRUCE WINERY**
'91, California, Vintner's Select $12.50

11 **GRANITE SPRINGS WINERY**
'91, El Dorado $10.00

9 **GUENOC WINERY**
'90, North Coast $13.00

9 **HOP KILN WINERY**
'91, Sonoma Co. $15.00

9 **TRENTADUE**
'91, Sonoma Co. $11.00

9 **WINDSOR VINEYARDS**
'90, North Coast $10.00

8 **ROSENBLUM CELLARS**
'91, Napa Vly. $12.00

8 **GRANITE SPRINGS WINERY**
'90, El Dorado Co., Granite Hill $10.00

6 **FETZER VINEYARDS**
'90, Mendocino Co., Reserve

Petite Sirah	L.A.	Orange Farmers	San Fran	Dallas	State Fair	New World	W. Coast	San Diego
6 AWARDS								
CHRISTOPHER CREEK '90, Russian River Vly. $13.00	S	G	B	S	G			B
5 AWARDS								
GUENOC WINERY '90, North Coast $13.00	B	S			B		S	B
HOP KILN WINERY '91, Sonoma Co. $15.00	B	B	S		S			B
4 AWARDS								
RABBIT RIDGE VINEYARDS '90, Sonoma Co. $9.50		G	S				S	B
ROSENBLUM CELLARS '91, Napa Vly. $12.00		S	B		S		B	
3 AWARDS								
DAVID BRUCE WINERY '91, California, Vintner's Select $12.50	B	G					G	
GRANITE SPRINGS WINERY '91, El Dorado $10.00		S		S	G			
GUENOC WINERY '89, North Coast $13.00			S		B			B
IMAGERY SERIES '89, California $16.00	B	S	B					
STORRS WINERY '91, Santa Cruz Mtns. $14.00	B	B			S			
TRENTADUE '91, Sonoma Co. $11.00	B	G			S			
WINDSOR VINEYARDS '90, North Coast $10.00	G			S	B			
2 AWARDS								
ARCIERO WINERY '89, Paso Robles, Estate $7.50			S	B				
BLACK MOUNTAIN VINEYARD '90, Alexander Vly., Bosun Crest $10.00			B		B			
CHOUINARD VINEYARDS '91, Napa Vly. $11.00			B					B
CILURZO VINEYARD '90, Temecula, Prop. Reserve $12.00			B					B
FETZER VINEYARDS '90, Mendocino Co., Reserve				S	S			

L.A.	Orange Farmers	San Fran	Dallas	State Fair	New World	W. Coast	San Diego	
					S	B		**GEYSER PEAK WINERY** '90, Alexander Vly. $15.00
B	Σ							**GRANITE SPRINGS WINERY** '90, El Dorado Co., Granite Hill $10.00
	B	S						**GUENOC WINERY** '88, Guenoc Vly.
				S		B		**PARDUCCI WINE CELLARS** '89, Mendocino Co. $6.00
B						B		**WINDSOR VINEYARDS** 'NV, Sonoma Co. $9.50

2 AWARDS

Fifth Generation Harvest Reserve

Mirassou

1991
Monterey County

Pinot Blanc
Limited Bottling

PRODUCED AND BOTTLED BY
MIRASSOU VINEYARDS, SAN JOSE, CALIFORNIA
ALCOHOL 13.5% BY VOLUME, 750 ML

Pinot Blanc

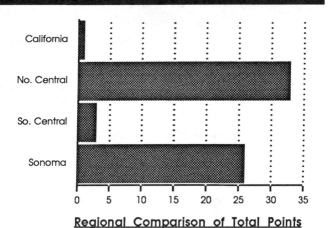

Regional Comparison of Total Points

(Gold-plus=7 Gold=5 Silver=3 Bronze=1)

Highest individual wine totals

26   **BENZIGER WINERY**
'91, Sonoma Co. $10.00

13   **MIRASSOU VINEYARDS**
'91, Monterey Co., Harvest Reserve $13.00

8   **MIRASSOU VINEYARDS**
'91, Monterey, Family Sel., Wt. Burgundy $7.50

4   **PARAISO SPRINGS VINEYARDS**
'91, Monterey Co. $8.00

3   **BYRON VINEYARD**
'92, Santa Barbara Co.

2   **ELLISTON VINEYARDS**
'91, Central Coast, Sunol Vly. Vnyd.

2   **MIRASSOU VINEYARDS**
'92, Monterey, Family Selection $7.00

2   **MIRASSOU VINEYARDS**
'90, Monterey Co., Harvest Reserve $12.00

BUTTERFLY CREEK WINERY
'91, California, LH $7.25

1   **GAVILAN**
'92, Monterey, Pinnacles, Soledad $12.50

1   **WILD HORSE WINERY**
'92, Monterey $12.00

Pinot Blanc

	L.A.	Orange Farmers	San Fran	Dallas	State Fair	New World	W. Coast	San Diego
6 AWARDS								
BENZIGER WINERY '91, Sonoma Co. $10.00	G	G	B			Σ	G	S
MIRASSOU VINEYARDS '91, Monterey, Family Selection, White Burgundy $7.50			S	B	B	B	B	B
5 AWARDS								
MIRASSOU VINEYARDS '91, Monterey Co., Limited Bottling $13.00	G	S	B			B		S
2 AWARDS								
ELLISTON VINEYARDS '91, Central Coast, Sunol Vly. Vnyd.						B		B
MIRASSOU VINEYARDS '92, Monterey, Family Selection $7.00				B	B			
MIRASSOU VINEYARDS '90, Monterey Co., Harvest Reserve $12.00				B		B		
PARAISO SPRINGS VINEYARDS '91, Monterey Co. $8.00		B						S

GARY FARRELL

1991
ALLEN VINEYARD
RUSSIAN RIVER VALLEY
PINOT NOIR

PRODUCED AND BOTTLED BY GARY FARRELL
HEALDSBURG CA · CONTAINS SULFITES · TABLE WINE

RODNEY STRONG

1991
River East Vineyard
Pinot Noir
RUSSIAN RIVER VALLEY

Pinot Noir

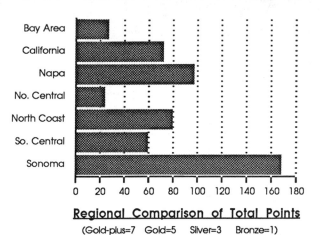

Regional Comparison of Total Points
(Gold-plus=7 Gold=5 Silver=3 Bronze=1)

Highest individual wine totals

34 **GARY FARRELL WINES**
'91, Russian River Vly., Allen Vnyd. $32.00

19 **RODNEY STRONG VINEYARDS**
'91, River East Vnyd. $14.00

18 **FETZER VINEYARDS**
'90, California, Reserve $19.00

16 **NAVARRO VINEYARDS**
'90, Anderson Vly., A'Lancienne $15.00

14 **FETZER VINEYARDS**
'91, California, Barrel Select $11.00

14 **KENDALL-JACKSON WINERY**
'91, Calif., Grand Reserve $30.00

12 **WINDSOR VINEYARDS**
'90, Russian River Vly. $10.00

12 **BEAULIEU VINEYARD**
'90, Napa, Carneros Reserve $17.00

11 **MERIDIAN VINEYARDS**
'90, Santa Barbara Co. $14.00

11 **GREENWOOD RIDGE VINEYARDS**
'91, Mendocino Co. $15.00

Pinot Noir

	L.A.	Orange Farmers	San Fran	Dallas	State Fair	New World	W. Coast	San Diego
8 AWARDS								
GARY FARRELL WINES '91, Russian River Vly., Allen Vnyd. $32.00	B	G	Σ	S	G	S	Σ	S
6 AWARDS								
FETZER VINEYARDS '90, California, Reserve $19.00	S			S	B	G	G	B
WINDSOR VINEYARDS '90, Russian River Vly. $10.00	B	B	B			G	B	S
5 AWARDS								
HANDLEY CELLARS '91, Anderson Vly. $12.50		S	B		B		S	B
MERIDIAN VINEYARDS '90, Santa Barbara Co. $14.00		B		S	S	S		B
RODNEY STRONG VINEYARDS '91, River East Vnyd. $14.00	B	S				G	G	G
4 AWARDS								
BEAULIEU VINEYARD '90, Napa, Carneros Reserve $17.00		B	B	G			G	
BENZIGER WINERY '90, Sonoma Co. $12.50	S	B			G			B
DAVID BRUCE WINERY '90, Santa Cruz Mtns., Reserve $30.00		S		B	B	B		
FETZER VINEYARDS '91, California, Barrel Select $11.00	G	G	B		S			
KENDALL-JACKSON WINERY '91, Calif., Grand Reserve $30.00		S	B		Σ			S
NAPA RIDGE '91, North Coast $7.50		B	B			Σ		B
NAVARRO VINEYARDS '90, Anderson Vly., A'Lancienne $15.00	S	Σ				S	S	
ROCHIOLI VINEYARD '91, Russian River Vly., Estate $18.00	G	B					B	B
WILD HORSE WINERY '91, Central Coast $16.00		G	B				S	B
ZACA MESA WINERY '90, Santa Barbara Co., Reserve $16.00	B	B		S			B	
3 AWARDS								
DAVIS BYNUM WINERY '90, Russian River Vly., Ltd. Release $18.00			B		B	B		

L.A.	Orange	Farmers	San Fran	Dallas	State Fair	New World	W. Coast	San Diego	Pinot Noir
						3 AWARDS			
					B	B	B		**CARNEROS CREEK WINERY** '91, Fleur de Carneros $10.00
G	S							S	**GREENWOOD RIDGE VINEYARDS** '91, Mendocino Co. $15.00
B			B			B			**KENDALL-JACKSON WINERY** '91, Calif., Vintner's Reserve $13.00
			B				S	G	**KENWOOD VINEYARDS** '91, Sonoma Mtn., Jack London $17.50
			B			S	S		**NAVARRO VINEYARDS** 'NV, Mendocino $9.00
						2 AWARDS			
			S				B		**ACACIA** '91, Napa, Carneros
			S	S					**ACACIA** '90, Napa, Carneros, St. Clair $21.00
G	G								**ARMIDA WINERY** '91, Russian River Vly.
				B		G			**BARGETTO WINERY** '90, Santa Cruz, Sessantesimo $15.00
			S	B					**DAVID BRUCE WINERY** '90, Santa Cruz Mtns., Estate
				B		B			**DAVID BRUCE WINERY** '90, California, Vintner's Select $12.50
						B	B		**DAVIS BYNUM WINERY** '91, Russian River Vly. $12.00
Σ	S								**CHATEAU DE LEU WINERY** '90, Napa Vly. $12.00
	B					B			**CHATEAU SOUVERAIN** '91, Carneros, Reserve $13.50
B			B						**CHEVAL SAUVAGE** '90, Paso Robles $28.00
S						B			**CLAUDIA SPRINGS WINERY** '91, Anderson Vly. $12.50
				B		B			**COSENTINO WINERY** '91, Carneros $18.00
	S					B			**CRESTON VINEYARDS** '91, Paso Robles $9.00

Pinot Noir

	L.A.	Orange Farmers	San Fran	Dallas	State Fair	New World	W. Coast	San Diego
2 AWARDS								
GARY FARRELL WINES '91, Russian River Vly. $16.50		B				G		
FIELDBROOK VALLEY WINERY '90, Napa Vly., Beard Vnyd. $12.00		B			B			
J. FURST '91, Sonoma Co. $9.00		B				G		
GAINEY VINEYARD '90, Santa Barbara Co. $15.00	B				B			
HUSCH VINEYARDS '90, Anderson Vly., Estate $14.00	G							G
LA CREMA WINERY '91, California, Reserve $19.00	S				G			
LOUIS M. MARTINI WINERY '90, Napa, La Loma Vnyd. $14.00	B				S			
MIRASSOU VINEYARDS '89, Monterey, Harvest Reserve $13.00		Σ B						
ROBERT MONDAVI WINERY '91, Napa Vly., Unfiltered $13.00		B						S
MONTICELLO CELLARS '90, Napa Vly., Estate $18.00				B				S
MORGAN '91, California $15.00		S			B			
NEWLAN VINEYARDS '89, Napa Vly. $18.00		S					B	
PARDUCCI WINE CELLARS '90, Mendocino $7.00					B	G		
J. PEDRONCELLI WINERY '90, Dry Creek Vly. $9.00		S						S
RICHARDSON VINEYARDS '91, Los Carneros, Sonoma Vly. $15.00		B						S
SANFORD WINERY '91, Santa Barbara Co. $16.00	Σ				S			
ROBERT SINSKEY VINEYARDS '91, Napa Vly., Los Carneros $19.00		B			S			
ROBERT STEMMLER WINERY '89, Sonoma Co. $20.00	S	B						
J. STONESTREET & SONS '91, Russian River Vly. $30.00	G				B			

L.A.	Orange	Farmers	San Fran	Dallas	State Fair	New World	W. Coast	San Diego	Pinot Noir
									2 AWARDS
						B	S		**TROUT GULCH VINEYARDS** '90, Santa Cruz Mtns. $20.00
B			B						**TRUCHARD VINEYARDS** '91, Napa Vly.
			B	G					**WESTWOOD WINERY** '91, California $10.00
			S				B		**WESTWOOD WINERY** '90, Napa Vly., Haynes Vnyd.
			G				S		**ZD WINES** '91, Napa Vly., Carneros $17.00

Estancia
Meritage

1990 VINTAGE
ESTANCIA ESTATES ALEXANDER VALLEY RED TABLE WINE
Alexander Valley

RESERVE ALEXANDRE

GEYSER PEAK

1990 Alexander Valley

Red Meritage

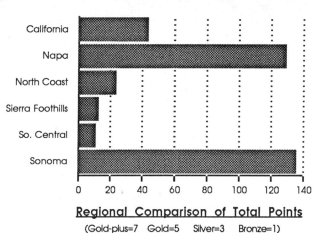

Regional Comparison of Total Points

(Gold-plus=7   Gold=5   Silver=3   Bronze=1)

Highest individual wine totals

32 — **ESTANCIA WINERY**
'90, Alexander Vly. $15.00

28 — **GEYSER PEAK WINERY**
'90, Reserve Alexandre $21.00

24 — **BENZIGER WINERY**
'89, Sonoma Mtn. "A Tribute" $27.00

18 — **LANGTRY**
'90, California $35.00

17 — **GOLDEN CREEK VINEYARD**
'90, Sonoma Co. Caberlot $12.00

17 — **MOUNT VEEDER WINERY**
'89, Napa Vly. $24.00

15 — **FRANCISCAN OAKVILLE ESTATE**
'89, Napa Vly. Magnificant $20.00

13 — **KATHRYN KENNEDY WINERY**
'91, California, Lateral $17.50

11 — **FLORA SPRINGS**
'89, Napa Vly., Trilogy $33.00

9 — **NEVADA CITY WINERY**
'90, Sierra Foothills, Director's Res. $14.00

Red Meritage	L.A.	Orange	Farmers	San Fran	Dallas	State Fair	New World	W. Coast	San Diego
8 AWARDS									
GEYSER PEAK WINERY '90, Reserve Alexandre $21.00	B		Σ	B	B	B	Σ	S	Σ
7 AWARDS									
FRANCISCAN OAKVILLE ESTATE '89, Napa Vly. Magnificant $20.00		B	B	S	B	S	B		G
GOLDEN CREEK VINEYARD '90, Sonoma Co. Caberlot $12.00	B		S	B	S	G	S	B	
MOUNT VEEDER WINERY '89, Napa Vly. $24.00			S	B	S	B	G	S	B
6 AWARDS									
BENZIGER WINERY '89, Sonoma Mtn. "A Tribute" $27.00	B		G	Σ			S	Σ	B
DE LORIMIER WINERY '88, Alexander Vly. Mosaic $18.00	B	S			B		B		B
ESTANCIA WINERY '90, Alexander Vly. $15.00	Σ		S	G	G			G	Σ
5 AWARDS									
KATHRYN KENNEDY WINERY '91, California, Lateral $17.50	B	S		S		G		B	
4 AWARDS									
GUENOC WINERY '89, Lake County $15.00				S	B	B			B
LANGTRY '90, California $35.00		G		G		G	S		
LANGTRY '89, Lake Co. $35.00				B	B		B		B
MERRYVALE VINEYARDS '89, Napa Vly., Profile $30.00	S	B			B	B			
ROMBAUER VINEYARDS '87, Napa, Le Meilleur Du Chai $35.00		G	B	B	B				
3 AWARDS									
COSENTINO WINERY '90, California, "The Poet" $25.00				B		B	S		
FLORA SPRINGS '89, Napa Vly., Trilogy $33.00		S			G	S			
NEVADA CITY WINERY '90, Sierra Foothills, Director's Reserve $14.00		G				B	S		

L.A.	Orange Farmers	San Fran	Dallas	State Fair	New World	W. Coast	San Diego	Red Meritage
								3 AWARDS
B		S		B				**SEBASTIANI VINEYARDS** '89, Sonoma, Red Hill Vineyard $14.00
								2 AWARDS
B		B						**CAIN CELLARS** '88, Napa Vly., Cuvee
	G	S						**THOMAS COYNE WINES** '90, Napa Vly., "Cabernets"
				B	G			**M. COZ** '90, Napa Vly. $45.00
		G		B				**DRY CREEK VINEYARD** '88, Dry Creek Vly. $24.00
B				B				**GUENOC WINERY** '88, Napa County/Lake County $35.00
				B			B	**JEKEL VINEYARDS** '89, Arroyo Seco, Symmetry $20.00
		S		B				**JUSTIN VINEYARDS** '89, Paso Robles Isosceles Res. $22.50
		G	S					**KENDALL-JACKSON WINERY** '88, California, Cardinale $50.00
B				B				**KONRAD ESTATE** '89, Melange a Trois $12.00
			B	S				**MAYA** '89, Napa Vly. $48.00
	G	S						**NAVARRO VINEYARDS** 'NV, Mendocino, Navarrouge
B	G							**QUIVIRA VINEYARDS** '89, Dry Creek Vly.,Cuvee
					B	B		**RANCHO SISQUOC** '89, Santa Maria Vly., Cellar Sel. $25.00

ESTATE BOTTLED

ROCHIOLI

1992

Sauvignon Blanc
Sonoma County

RUSSIAN RIVER VALLEY

ALC. 13.8% BY VOL.

GEYSER PEAK

SONOMA COUNTY
SAUVIGNON BLANC

ALC. 12.9% BY VOL.

Sauvignon Blanc

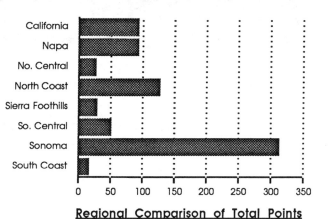

Regional Comparison of Total Points

(Gold-plus=7   Gold=5   Silver=3   Bronze=1)

Highest   individual wine totals

28	**ROCHIOLI VINEYARD** '92, Russian River Vly., Estate $11.00
25	**GEYSER PEAK WINERY** '92, Sonoma Co. $6.50
19	**ESTANCIA WINERY** '91, Monterey Co. $8.00
18	**DAVIS BYNUM WINERY** '92, Russian Riv., Shone Farm, Fume $8.50
17	**MURPHY-GOODE WINERY** '92, Alexander Vly., Fume $9.50
16	**BUENA VISTA WINERY** '92, Lake Co. $7.50
15	**GARY FARRELL WINES** '92, Russian River Rochioli Vnyd. $10.00
14	**DE LOACH VINEYARDS** '91, Russian River Vly. $10.00
14	**HANNA WINERY** '92, Sonoma Co. $9.65
14	**NAPA RIDGE** '91, North Coast $7.50
14	**ROBERT PEPI WINERY** '91, Napa Vly., Reserve Sel. $18.00

	L.A.	Orange	Farmers	San Fran	Dallas	State Fair	New World	W. Coast	San Diego
7 AWARDS									
GEYSER PEAK WINERY '92, Sonoma Co. $6.50	B	G	G		G	S	G	B	
6 AWARDS									
CORBETT CANYON VINEYARDS '92, Central Coast, Coastal Classic $4.50		B	S			B	B	S	S
HANDLEY CELLARS '91, Dry Creek Vly. $8.00		B		B	B		S	B	B
ROCHIOLI VINEYARD '92, Russian River Vly., Estate $11.00	G	B	S			Σ		Σ	G
5 AWARDS									
BAREFOOT CELLARS 'NV, California $4.00				B		B	B	B	S
CANYON ROAD CELLARS '92, California $4.75	B			B	B	G	B		
ESTANCIA WINERY '91, Monterey Co. $8.00	G					S	B	S	Σ
GARY FARRELL WINES '92, Russian River Rochioli Vnyd. $10.00	B		B			G	G	S	
GAINEY VINEYARD '91, Santa Ynez Vly. $9.00		S	B	S			S		S
GRGICH HILLS CELLAR '91, Napa Vly., Fume $11.00	S				B	B		B	S
HUSCH VINEYARDS '92, Mendocino, La Ribera Vnyd $8.50		B	S			B		S	S
KENWOOD VINEYARDS '91, Sonoma Co. $9.50		B		B	B	B			S
MURPHY-GOODE WINERY '92, Alexander Vly., Fume $9.50		G	B			B		G	G
ST. CLEMENT VINEYARDS '92, Napa Vly. $10.50		S	B	B		B		B	
TAFT STREET WINERY '91, Sonoma Co. $6.00		B		B			S	S	S
4 AWARDS									
ALDERBROOK WINERY '91, Dry Creek Vly., Estate $7.50				B		S		B	B
BUENA VISTA WINERY '92, Lake Co. $7.50	S	G		S		G			
BUENA VISTA WINERY '91, Lake Co. $7.50		B	S			S	G		

L.A.	Orange	Farmers	San Fran	Dallas	State Fair	New World	W. Coast	San Diego	Sauvignon Blanc
					4 AWARDS				
G	S		G			G			**DAVIS BYNUM WINERY** '92, Russian Riv., Shone Farm, Fume $8.50
S	B					B	B		**CLOS DU BOIS** '92, Alexander Vly., Barrel Ferm. $8.00
S		S				G		S	**DE LOACH VINEYARDS** '91, Russian River Vly. $10.00
S	B			B		S			**DRY CREEK VINEYARD** '91, Sonoma Co., Fume $9.25
S		B	B			B			**J. FURST** '91, California, Fume $9.00
	B	G	B	B					**GREENWOOD RIDGE VINEYARDS** '91, Anderson Vly. $8.50
	Σ		S	B		S			**HANNA WINERY** '92, Sonoma Co. $9.65
	B			B		B	B		**KENDALL-JACKSON WINERY** '91, Calif., Vintner's Reserve $9.00
	B	S		S		B			**KONOCTI WINERY** '91, Lake Co., Fume $7.50
	Σ			B		G			**NAPA RIDGE** '91, North Coast $7.50
B	S		S						**OBESTER WINERY** '91, Mendocino Co. $9.00
		B				G		S	**ROBERT PEPI WINERY** '91, Napa Vly., Reserve Sel. $18.00
					3 AWARDS				
				B		B			**AUSTIN CELLARS** '91, Santa Barbara, Lucas Vnyd. $9.00
					S	B			**BENZIGER WINERY** '91, Sonoma Mtn., Estate $13.50
						S	B		**BERINGER VINEYARDS** '91, Napa Vly., Fume $9.00
		B				B	B		**CALLAWAY VINEYARD** '91, Temecula, Fume $8.00
	B		B			S			**DE LOACH VINEYARDS** '91, Russian River Vly., Fume $10.00
B	B					S			**GRAND CRU VINEYARDS** '91, California $6.50

Sauvignon Blanc

	L.A.	Orange	Farmers	San Fran	Dallas	State Fair	New World	W. Coast	San Diego
3 AWARDS									
GUENOC WINERY '91, Guenoc Vly., Estate $10.00	B	B		S					
JEPSON VINEYARDS '90, Mendocino $8.50		B	B						S
MONTEVINA WINES '91, California, Fume $6.50		G			G		S		
R. H. PHILLIP VINEYARD '92, California $6.00					B	B	B		
QUAIL RIDGE CELLARS '91, Napa Vly. $8.00		B				B			B
ST. SUPERY WINERY '91, Napa Vly., Dollarhide Ranch $9.00		B				B	S		
WINDSOR VINEYARDS '92, Sonoma Co., Fume $7.50	B		G					B	
2 AWARDS									
ADLER FELS WINERY '91, Sonoma Co., Fume $9.00							B		S
AMADOR FOOTHILL WINERY '91, Shenandoah Vly., Fume $8.00	S						S		
BENZIGER WINERY '91, Sonoma Co., Fume $9.00		G	S						
BOEGER WINERY '91, El Dorado, Estate $7.50	B	B							
BRANDER VINEYARD '91, Santa Ynez Vly. $9.75			S						B
BRICELAND VINEYARDS '92, Humboldt Co. $9.50		B				S			
CAREY CELLARS '91, Santa Ynez Vly. $8.00			S						B
MAURICE CARRIE WINERY '91, Temecula $5.00						B			S
CHALK HILL WINERY '91, Sonoma Co., Estate $10.00		B						S	
CHATEAU ST. JEAN '91, Russian River, Fume $11.00								B	B
COTES DE SONOMA '92, Sonoma Co. $6.00		G				S			
FALLENLEAF WINERY '91, Sonoma Vly. $9.00					B	B			

L.A.	Orange Farmers	San Fran Dallas	State Fair	New World W. Coast	San Diego	
				2 AWARDS		
			B	S		**FETZER VINEYARDS** '92, California Fume $7.00
B			B			**J. FRITZ WINERY** '92, Dry Creek Vly. $8.00
	B			B		**GLEN ELLEN WINERY** '92, California $4.99
B				S		**GUENOC WINERY** '90, Guenoc Vly., Estate $10.00
				B		**HANNA WINERY** '90, Sonoma Co. $9.65
		S		S		**HIDDEN CELLARS** '91, California $9.00
			B	G		**JOULLIAN VINEYARD** '91, Carmel Vly. $6.50
			B			**KARLY WINERY** '91, Amador Co. $9.00
		G		B		**KENDALL-JACKSON WINERY** '92, California, Vintner's Reserve
	S	B				**KORBEL** '91, Alexander Vly.
		Σ		S		**LAKESPRING WINERY** '92, Napa Vly., Yount Mill Vnyd. $8.50
	S			S		**LIMERICK LANE** '92, Russian River, Collins Vnyd. $7.00
	G			B		**LOLONIS WINERY** '91, Mendocino Co., Fume $8.50
		B		G		**M. MARION** '92, Sonoma Co. $7.00
				B		**MARKHAM VINEYARDS** '91, Napa Vly. $8.00
				G	B	**MERIDIAN VINEYARDS** '92, California $8.25
		S		B		**MIRASSOU VINEYARDS** '91, California $5.00
	B			S		**NAVARRO VINEYARDS** '91, Mendocino, Cuvee 128 $9.75
		B	B			**J. PEDRONCELLI WINERY** '91, Dry Creek Vly., Fume $8.00

Sauvignon Blanc	L.A. Orange Farmers	San Fran Dallas State Fair	New World W. Coast San Diego
2 AWARDS			
SANFORD WINERY '91, Santa Barbara Co.			B B
SANTINO WINES '89, Le Lou-Bricant, SLH $18.00	G	S	
V. SATTUI WINERY '92, Suzanne's Vnyd., Estate			S B
SEGHESIO WINERY '92, Dry Creek Vly. $8.00		S	G
SIERRA VISTA WINERY '92, El Dorado $7.50	B		S
SILVERADO VINEYARDS '92, Napa Vly.	B	B	
STONE CREEK CELLARS '91, Napa, Fume, Special Sel. $6.25	S		B
RODNEY STRONG VINEYARDS '92, Charlotte's Home Vnyd. $9.00	B		B
VENTANA VINEYARDS '91, Monterey Co., Estate $8.00	B		S
WHITE OAK VINEYARDS '92, Sonoma Co. $8.95	B		S

GEYSER PEAK

SEMCHARD
CALIFORNIA
75% SEMILLON, 25% CHARDONNAY

ALC. 13.1% BY VOL.

1990 ESTATE BOTTLED

LACE

ALEXANDER VALLEY
LATE HARVEST SEMILLON

ALC. 10.8% BY VOL.

Semillon

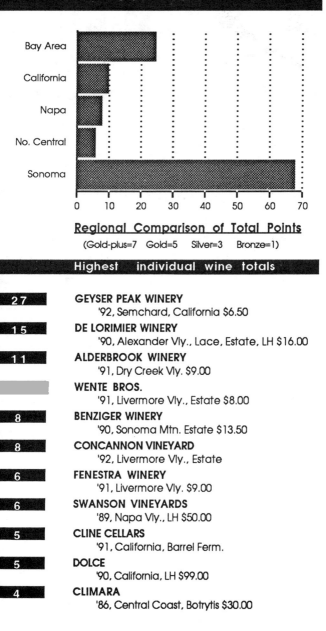

Regional Comparison of Total Points
(Gold-plus=7   Gold=5   Silver=3   Bronze=1)

Highest   individual   wine   totals

27   **GEYSER PEAK WINERY**
'92, Semchard, California $6.50

15   **DE LORIMIER WINERY**
'90, Alexander Vly., Lace, Estate, LH $16.00

11   **ALDERBROOK WINERY**
'91, Dry Creek Vly. $9.00

WENTE BROS.
'91, Livermore Vly., Estate $8.00

8   **BENZIGER WINERY**
'90, Sonoma Mtn. Estate $13.50

8   **CONCANNON VINEYARD**
'92, Livermore Vly., Estate

6   **FENESTRA WINERY**
'91, Livermore Vly. $9.00

6   **SWANSON VINEYARDS**
'89, Napa Vly., LH $50.00

5   **CLINE CELLARS**
'91, California, Barrel Ferm.

5   **DOLCE**
'90, California, LH $99.00

4   **CLIMARA**
'86, Central Coast, Botrytis $30.00

Semillon	L.A.	Orange	Farmers	San Fran	Dallas	State Fair	New World	W. Coast	San Diego
9 AWARDS									
GEYSER PEAK WINERY '92, Semchard, California $6.50	G	S	G	B	B	B	G	S	S
5 AWARDS									
ALDERBROOK WINERY '91, Dry Creek Vly. $9.00		B	G	B				S	B
DE LORIMIER WINERY '90, Alexander Vly., Lace, Estate, LH $16.00	B	G		B	S				G
WENTE BROS. '91, Livermore Vly., Estate $8.00		S	G			B	B	B	
4 AWARDS									
FENESTRA WINERY '91, Livermore Vly. $9.00		S	B	B					B
3 AWARDS									
CLINE CELLARS '91, California, Barrel Ferm.							B	B	S
2 AWARDS									
BENZIGER WINERY '90, Sonoma Mtn. Estate $13.50			B				Σ		
CLIMARA '86, Central Coast, Botrytis $30.00		S		B					
CONCANNON VINEYARD '92, Livermore Vly., Estate	B					Σ			
LAKEWOOD VINEYARDS '91, Clear Lake $12.00		B		B					
SWANSON VINEYARDS '89, Napa Vly., LH $50.00		S							S

MUMM

CUVÉE NAPA

BLANC DE NOIRS

METHODE CHAMPENOISE

NAPA VALLEY SPARKLING WINE

750 ML (25.4 FL OZ)   ALC. 12.5% BY VOL.

GLORIA FERRER

FERMENTED IN
THIS BOTTLE

SONOMA COUNTY
SPARKLING WINE

PRODUCED AND BOTTLED
BY FREIXENET SONOMA CAVES
SONOMA, CALIFORNIA

ALCOHOL 12%
BY VOLUME
750 ML

Gloria Ferrer

BRUT

SONOMA COUNTY MÉTHODE CHAMPENOISE

Sparkling Wine

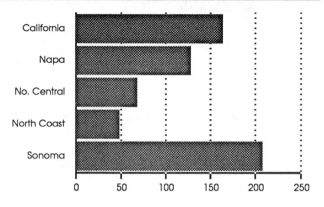

Regional Comparison of Total Points

(Gold-plus=7   Gold=5   Silver=3   Bronze=1)

Highest   individual   wine totals

33 **MUMM CUVEE NAPA**
'NV, Napa Vly., Blanc de Noirs $14.00

26 **BALLATORE CHAMPAGNE**
'NV, California Gran Spumante $5.50

25 **GLORIA FERRER**
'NV, Sonoma Co., Brut $14.00

25 **VAN DER KAMP CHAMPAGNE**
'88, Sonoma Vly., Brut $14.50

24 **S. ANDERSON VINEYARD**
'87, Napa Vly., Brut $18.00

21 **MAISON DEUTZ WINERY**
'NV, SLO/S. Barbara, Brut Cuvee $15.00

17 **S. ANDERSON VINEYARD**
'88, Napa Vly., Blanc de Noirs $20.00

17 **CHATEAU ST. JEAN**
'NV, Sonoma, Blanc de Blanc $12.00

17 **MUMM CUVEE NAPA**
'89, Carneros, Winery Lake Brut $18.00

16 **MIRASSOU VINEYARDS**
'89, Monterey Co. Au Natural $13.00

16 **NAVARRO VINEYARDS**
'88, Mendocino, Brut $16.50

Sparkling Wine
0 – 1.5 Residual Sugar

9 AWARDS

Wine	L.A.	Orange	Farmers	San Fran	Dallas	State Fair	New World	W. Coast	San Diego
GLORIA FERRER — 'NV, Sonoma Co., Brut $14.00	G	S	S	B	S	G	B	S	B
MUMM CUVEE NAPA — 'NV, Napa Vly., Blanc de Noirs $14.00	S	G	Σ	G	B	G	B	S	S

8 AWARDS

Wine	L.A.	Orange	Farmers	San Fran	Dallas	State Fair	New World	W. Coast	San Diego
S. ANDERSON VINEYARD — '87, Napa Vly., Brut $18.00	G	B	B	B	G	G		S	S

7 AWARDS

Wine	L.A.	Orange	Farmers	San Fran	Dallas	State Fair	New World	W. Coast	San Diego
S. ANDERSON VINEYARD — '88, Napa Vly., Blanc de Noirs $20.00		S	B	S	S	S		S	B
CHATEAU ST. JEAN — 'NV, Sonoma, Blanc de Blanc $12.00	S			S	S	B	S	S	B
MAISON DEUTZ WINERY — 'NV, SLO/S. Barbara, Brut Cuvee $15.00	G		S		S	S	S	S	B
MIRASSOU VINEYARDS — '90, Monterey, Blanc de Noirs $13.00		S		B	B	B	B	B	G
MUMM CUVEE NAPA — 'NV, Napa Vly., Brut Prestige $14.00		S		B	B	S	B	G	B
VAN DER KAMP CHAMPAGNE — '88, Sonoma Vly., Brut $14.50	G	S	B	G	B	G			G

6 AWARDS

Wine	L.A.	Orange	Farmers	San Fran	Dallas	State Fair	New World	W. Coast	San Diego
KORBEL — 'NV, California, Natural $13.00	G			B	B	B		S	B
MIRASSOU VINEYARDS — '89, Monterey Co. Au Natural $13.00	S			S	B	G	B		S
WINDSOR VINEYARDS — '88, Sonoma Co., Blanc de Blanc $17.50	S	S		B		S		B	B
WINDSOR VINEYARDS — '88, Sonoma Co., Blanc de Noir $13.33	B	B		B	B			S	B

5 AWARDS

Wine	L.A.	Orange	Farmers	San Fran	Dallas	State Fair	New World	W. Coast	San Diego
KORBEL — 'NV, California, Blanc de Noirs $13.00		S		B	B	S	B		
MIRASSOU VINEYARDS — '90, Monterey, Brut $13.00	S	B				B	B	G	
MIRASSOU VINEYARDS — '85, Monterey Co., Reserve, Brut $15.00	G			S			B	S	S
MUMM CUVEE NAPA — '89, Carneros, Winery Lake Brut $18.00	S	S		S		G			S

L.A.	Orange Farmers	San Fran	Dallas	State Fair	New World	W. Coast	San Diego	Sparkling Wine — 0-1.5 Residual Sugar
B		S	B		B		S	**VAN DER KAMP CHAMPAGNE** '89, Sonoma Vly., Midnight Cuvee $14.50
B		S	B		B	B		**WINDSOR VINEYARDS** '88, Sonoma Co., Brut Rose $12.00
				4 AWARDS				
B	B	S			B			**CHATEAU ST. JEAN** 'NV, Sonoma Co. Brut $12.00
B	G			S			B	**GLORIA FERRER** '87, Carneros, Royal Cuvee $17.00
B	G			B			Σ	**GLORIA FERRER** '86, Carneros, Carneros Cuvee $23.00
		S			B	S	G	**MAISON DEUTZ WINERY** 'NV, SLO/S. Barbara, Brut Rose $24.00
	S	Σ			B	G		**NAVARRO VINEYARDS** '88, Mendocino, Brut $16.50
				3 AWARDS				
B	Σ			B				**BENZIGER WINERY** '88, Sonoma, Blanc de Blancs $12.00
				B	S	G		**CORDONIU NAPA** 'NV, Napa Vly. Brut $15.00
		B		S			G	**HANDLEY CELLARS** '88, Anderson Vly., Blanc de Blanc $18.00
G	S						Σ	**J** '89, Sonoma Co. Brut $23.00
B				B	B			**JEPSON VINEYARDS** '88, Mendocino, Blanc de Blanc $16.00
B				S	S			**WENTE BROS.** 'NV, Arroyo Seco, Grande Brut $10.00
				2 AWARDS				
						S	B	**BARGETTO WINERY** '91, Santa Maria, Blanc De Noir $11.00
		B			S			**CALLAWAY VINEYARD** '88, Temecula, Blanc de Blanc $16.00
S					B			**CHATEAU DE BAUN WINERY** 'NV, Sonoma Co. Brut $12.00
B	B							**CHATEAU DE BAUN WINERY** 'NV, Sonoma Co. Brut Rose $12.00

Sparkling Wine
0 - 1.5 Residual Sugar

	L.A. Orange Farmers	San Fran	Dallas	State Fair	New World W. Coast	San Diego
2 AWARDS						
CULBERTSON WINERY '87, California, Brut $16.00		B			G	
CULBERTSON WINERY 'NV, California, Cuvee Rouge $12.00	B					S
CULBERTSON WINERY '87, California, Natural $16.00					B	S
CULBERTSON WINERY '87, California, Brut Rose				B		B
RICHARD CUNEO '88, Sonoma, Blanc de Blanc $14.00		S	G			
HANDLEY CELLARS '89, Anderson Vly., Brut Rose	S			S		
HANDLEY CELLARS '88, Anderson Vly., Brut $15.00		S				S
J '88, Sonoma Co. $23.00				G	G	
MAISON DEUTZ WINERY 'NV, SLO/S. Barbara, Blanc de Noir $16.00	G	B				

L.A.	Orange Farmers	San Fran	Dallas	State Fair	New World	W. Coast	San Diego	Sparkling Wine 1.6+ Residual Sugar
								6 AWARDS
S		Σ		B	G	G	G	**BALLATORE CHAMPAGNE** 'NV, California Gran Spumante $5.50
								5 AWARDS
B	G	B	S		B			**COOK'S CHAMPAGNE CELLARS** 'NV, American Spumante $3.99
								3 AWARDS
			B		B	S		**COOK'S CHAMPAGNE CELLARS** 'NV, American, Imperial, Blush $3.99
S		B	B					**CULBERTSON WINERY** 'NV, Calif., Cuvee de Frontignan $12.00
								2 AWARDS
		S					B	**COOK'S CHAMPAGNE CELLARS** 'NV, American, Grand Reserve $3.99
					B	B		**COOK'S CHAMPAGNE CELLARS** 'NV, American, Imperial, Brut $3.99
		B				S		**COOK'S CHAMPAGNE CELLARS** 'NV, American, Imperial, Extra Dry $3.99
		B	B					**KORBEL** 'NV, California Rouge $11.00
B		B						**KORBEL** 'NV, California, Brut $13.00
		S	B					**KORBEL** 'NV, California, Extra Dry $11.00

CHRISTOPHER CREEK

ESTATE BOTTLED

1990

RUSSIAN RIVER VALLEY

SYRAH

SONOMA COUNTY

GROWN, PRODUCED, AND BOTTLED BY
SOTOYOME WINERY
LIMERICK LANE, HEALDSBURG, CALIFORNIA
ALCOHOL 12.8% BY VOLUME. CONTAINS SULFITES

GEYSER PEAK

1991 Alexander Valley Syrah

Syrah

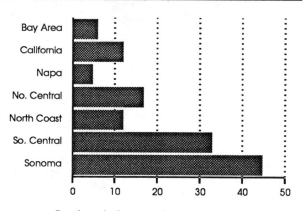

Regional Comparison of Total Points

(Gold-plus=7   Gold=5   Silver=3   Bronze=1)

Highest individual wine totals

23   **CHRISTOPHER CREEK**
'90, Russian River Vly., Estate $14.00

17   **GEYSER PEAK WINERY**
'91, Alexander Vly., Reserve $12.00

16   **RIVER RUN**
'91, Monterey Co., Ventana Vnyd. $11.00

11   **MERIDIAN VINEYARDS**
'90, Paso Robles $14.00

11   **ZACA MESA WINERY**
'91, Santa Barbara Co. $12.00

8   **EBERLE WINERY**
'91, Paso Robles $12.00

6   **CLINE CELLARS**
'91, Contra Costa Co. $14.50

6   **KENDALL-JACKSON WINERY**
'89, Sonoma Vly., Durell Vnyd.

5   **R. H. PHILLIP VINEYARD**
'89, California, EXP

5   **IMAGERY SERIES**
'90,

5   **MC DOWELL VALLEY VINEYARDS**
'90, Les Vieux Cepages

4   **KENDALL-JACKSON WINERY**
'90, California, Vintner's Reserve $13.00

Syrah

		L.A.	Orange Farmers	San Fran	Dallas	State Fair	New World	W. Coast	San Diego
7 AWARDS									
CHRISTOPHER CREEK '90, Russian River Vly., Estate $14.00			Σ	S	B	S	S	G	B
MERIDIAN VINEYARDS '90, Paso Robles $14.00		S	B	S	B	B		B	B
5 AWARDS									
GEYSER PEAK WINERY '91, Alexander Vly., Reserve $12.00		G	S	S		G	B		
ZACA MESA WINERY '91, Santa Barbara Co. $12.00		S	B	B		S			S
4 AWARDS									
CLINE CELLARS '91, Contra Costa Co. $14.50			B	B		S	B		
RIVER RUN '91, Monterey Co., Ventana Vnyd. $11.00		S	S	G				G	
3 AWARDS									
R. H. PHILLIP VINEYARD '89, California, EXP						B		S	
2 AWARDS									
EBERLE WINERY '91, Paso Robles $12.00							S	G	
KENDALL-JACKSON WINERY '90, California, Vintner's Reserve $13.00				B					
KENDALL-JACKSON WINERY '89, Sonoma Vly., Durell Vnyd.						S	S		

Knights Valley

ESTABLISHED 1876

Beringer.
1991

KNIGHTS VALLEY
Sauvignon Blanc & Semillon
Meritage
PROPRIETOR GROWN

*Our Knights Valley Meritage wine is made from
56% Sauvignon Blanc and 44% Semillon.*

HIDDEN CELLARS

ALCHEMY

Mendocino County
White Table Wine
1991

ALC 11.8%
BY VOL.

White Meritage

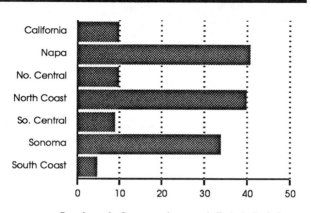

Regional Comparison of Total Points

(Gold-plus=7 Gold=5 Silver=3 Bronze=1)

Highest individual wine totals

22 **BERINGER VINEYARDS**
'91, Knights Vly. $9.00

15 **HIDDEN CELLARS**
'91, Mendocino Co., Alchemy $18.00

10 **ESTANCIA WINERY**
'91, Monterey $12.00

10 **KENDALL-JACKSON WINERY**
'91, California, Royale $15.00

10 **KONOCTI WINERY**
'91, Clear Lake, Mt. Konocti, Select $14.00

9 **ALDERBROOK WINERY**
'92, Dry Creek Vly., "Duet" $12.00

9 **DE LORIMIER WINERY**
'90, Alexander Vly., Spectrum $10.00

8 **LANGTRY**
'90, Guenoc Vly. $17.00

8 **RABBIT RIDGE VINEYARDS**
'91, Sonoma Co., Mystique $7.00

7 **BENZIGER WINERY**
'90, Sonoma Mtn., "A Tribute" $15.00

7 **MERRYVALE VINEYARDS**
'92, Napa Vly. $13.00

7 **BRANDER VINEYARD**
'91, Tete De Cuvee

White Meritage

White Meritage	L.A.	Orange Farmers	San Fran	Dallas	State Fair	New World	W. Coast	San Diego
8 AWARDS								
BERINGER VINEYARDS '91, Knights Vly. $9.00	S	S	S	G	S	S	B	B
5 AWARDS								
HIDDEN CELLARS '91, Mendocino Co., Alchemy $18.00		G	S	B			G	B
4 AWARDS								
ESTANCIA WINERY '91, Monterey $12.00	S		B	B		G		
KENDALL-JACKSON WINERY '91, California, Royale $15.00	B	G	B		S			
KONOCTI WINERY '91, Clear Lake, Mt. Konocti, Select $14.00	S	B			B		G	
VICHON WINERY '91, Napa Vly., Chevrignon $9.60		S	B				B	B
3 AWARDS								
ALDERBROOK WINERY '92, Dry Creek Vly., "Duet" $12.00			G	B			S	
BENZIGER WINERY '90, Sonoma Mtn., "A Tribute" $15.00			G	B				B
DE LORIMIER WINERY '90, Alexander Vly., Spectrum $10.00	S	G		B				
MERRYVALE VINEYARDS '92, Napa Vly. $13.00		S	S	B				
2 AWARDS								
CONCANNON VINEYARD '91, Livermore Vly., Assemblage $14.95			B	B				
LANGTRY '90, Guenoc Vly. $17.00			G		S			
RABBIT RIDGE VINEYARDS '91, Sonoma Co., Mystique $7.00			S				G	
WILDHURST VINEYARDS '91, Clear Lake Matillaha $16.00				B				B

HARMONY CELLARS

1992

White Zinfandel

PASO ROBLES

PRODUCED & BOTTLED BY HARMONY WINERY
PASO ROBLES, CALIFORNIA ALCOHOL 10.3% BY VOLUME

White Zinfandel

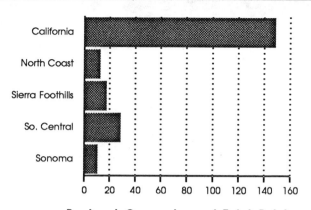

Regional Comparison of Total Points

(Gold-plus=7 Gold=5 Silver=3 Bronze=1)

Highest individual wine totals

25 **GLEN ELLEN WINERY**
'92, California, Prop. Reserve $5.00

19 **HARMONY CELLARS**
'92, Paso Robles $6.00

17 **M. G. VALLEJO WINERY**
'92, Calif., Harvest Select $6.00

14 **GRAND CRU VINEYARDS**
'92, California $6.50

11 **J. FURST**
'92, California $7.00

11 **V. SATTUI WINERY**
'92, California $7.50

10 **MONTPELLIER VINEYARDS**
'92, California

10 **BERINGER VINEYARDS**
'92, North Coast $6.00

9 **ESTRELLA RIVER**
'92, California $4.50

8 **SANTINO WINES**
'89, Amador, DBS White Harvest $14.00

7 **SANTINO WINES**
'92, Amador Co., White Harvest $6.00

7 **J. PEDRONCELLI WINERY**
'92, Sonoma Co. Rose $5.50

White Zinfandel

White Zinfandel	L.A.	Orange Farmers	San Fran	Dallas	State Fair	New World	W. Coast	San Diego
7 AWARDS								
GLEN ELLEN WINERY '92, California, Prop. Reserve $5.00	G	G	B		S	B	G	G
M. G. VALLEJO WINERY '92, Calif., Harvest Select $6.00	G	S	S	B	S		B	B
6 AWARDS								
GRAND CRU VINEYARDS '92, California $6.50			B	S	B	S	S	S
5 AWARDS								
BEL ARBORS '92, California, Founder's Sel. $5.00			B		B	B	B	B
HARMONY CELLARS '92, Paso Robles $6.00	G	B			G	G	S	
4 AWARDS								
BARON HERZOG WINE CELLARS '92, California					B	B	S	B
BERINGER VINEYARDS '92, North Coast $6.00			B	S	S			S
CASTORO CELLARS '92, San Luis Obispo $6.00	B		B				B	B
MONTPELLIER VINEYARDS '92, California					G	B	B	S
3 AWARDS								
CRESTON VINEYARDS '92, Paso Robles $6.00			B		B	B		
ESTRELLA RIVER '92, California $4.50			B		S	G		
FETZER VINEYARDS '92, California $6.75			B		B	S		
J. FURST '92, California $7.00			B	Σ		S		
J. PEDRONCELLI WINERY '92, Sonoma Co. Rose $5.50			B	S	S			
R. H. PHILLIP VINEYARD '92, California $5.00					B	B	B	
SANTINO WINES '92, Amador Co., White Harvest $6.00			B		B			G
V. SATTUI WINERY '92, California $7.50	S	S			G			

L.A.	Orange Farmers	San Fran	Dallas	State Fair	New World	W. Coast	San Diego	White Zinfandel
					3 AWARDS			
		B			S		B	**VENDANGE** '92, California $6.00
					2 AWARDS			
			B		B			**DE LOACH VINEYARDS** '92, Russian River Vly. $7.50
B					B			**MONTEREY VINEYARD** '92, Monterey Co. Classic $5.00
			B	B				**NAPA RIDGE** '92, Lodi $6.00
		S			G			**SANTINO WINES** '89, Amador, DBS White Harvest $14.00
B					B			**STONE CREEK CELLARS** '92, California $5.50
			B		B			**TWIN HILLS RANCH WINERY** 'NV, Paso Robles Rose $5.50
	B				B			**WINDSOR VINEYARDS** '92, Sonoma Co. $7.00

GARY FARRELL

1991
SONOMA COUNTY
RUSSIAN RIVER VALLEY
ZINFANDEL

PRODUCED AND BOTTLED BY GARY FARRELL
HEALDSBURG CA. CONTAINS SULFITES. TABLE WINE

Zinfandel

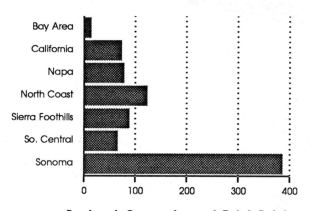

Regional Comparison of Total Points

(Gold-plus=7 Gold=5 Silver=3 Bronze=1)

Highest individual wine totals

28 — **GARY FARRELL WINES**
'91, Russian River Vly. $14.50

24 — **RABBIT RIDGE VINEYARDS**
'91, Dry Creek Vly. $9.50

21 — **HOP KILN WINERY**
'91, Russian River Vly., LH $15.00

19 — **LIMERICK LANE**
'91, Russian River Vly. $12.00

17 — **HOP KILN WINERY**
'91, Sonoma Co., Primitivo $15.00

16 — **KONRAD ESTATE**
'90, Mendocino Co. $8.50

16 — **TRENTADUE**
'90, Alexander Vly. $10.00

15 — **SAUCELITO CANYON**
'91, Arroyo Grande Vly., Estate $12.00

15 — **BERINGER VINEYARDS**
'89, Napa Co. $8.50

14 — **PERRY CREEK VINEYARDS**
'90, El Dorado Co. $8.00

Zinfandel

	L.A.	Orange	Farmers	San Fran	Dallas	State Fair	New World	W. Coast	San Diego
8 AWARDS									
GARY FARRELL WINES '91, Russian River Vly. $14.50	G	G	B	S	G	G		B	S
7 AWARDS									
BERINGER VINEYARDS '89, Napa Co. $8.50		B	B	S	S		S	B	S
6 AWARDS									
PERRY CREEK VINEYARDS '90, El Dorado Co. $8.00	S	B		S		S	S		B
RABBIT RIDGE VINEYARDS '91, Dry Creek Vly. $9.50	G		S		G		G	B	G
5 AWARDS									
CASTORO CELLARS '90, Paso Robles $9.00	G	G	B	B					B
CLINE CELLARS '91, Contra Costa Co. $9.00	S	B				B		B	B
GRANITE SPRINGS WINERY '90, El Dorado Co., Estate $8.50	B	G					S	B	S
HOP KILN WINERY '91, Russian River Vly., LH $15.00		G	Σ			G	S		B
HOP KILN WINERY '91, Sonoma Co., Primitivo $15.00	G		S	S	S				S
HOP KILN WINERY '90, Sonoma Co. $12.00	S	B		G	B				S
KENDALL-JACKSON WINERY '89, Mendocino Co., Ciapusci $20.00		S	B		S	S			B
LIMERICK LANE '91, Russian River Vly. $12.00		S		G	G		B	G	
ROUND HILL CELLARS '90, Napa Vly. $7.00		B			S	B	S		B
4 AWARDS									
BENZIGER WINERY '90, Sonoma Co. $10.00	B	B						G	B
BURGESS CELLARS '90, Napa Vly. $10.00	B			B	B				B
CHATEAU SOUVERAIN '90, Dry Creek Vly. $8.00						S	B	S	B
DRY CREEK VINEYARD '90, Dry Creek Vly., Old Vines $11.00		B			B		B		G

L.A.	Orange Farmers	San Fran	Dallas	State Fair	New World	W. Coast	San Diego	**Zinfandel**
								4 AWARDS
	B	B	S	S				**FETZER VINEYARDS** '90, Mendocino, Barrel Select $9.00
B	B			B			B	**FRANCISCAN OAKVILLE ESTATE** '91, Napa Vly. $10.00
B		S		B	B			**GRGICH HILLS CELLAR** '89, Sonoma Co. $13.00
		B	B		S	S		**HIDDEN CELLARS** '90, Mendocino Co. $11.00
B		B				B	G	**KENDALL-JACKSON WINERY** '91, California, Vintner's Reserve $10.00
		S			B	B	B	**KENDALL-JACKSON WINERY** '89, Anderson Vly., DuPratt Vnyd. $16.00
G	Σ	S			B			**KONRAD ESTATE** '90, Mendocino Co. $8.50
Σ		S		B	B			**A. RAFANELLI WINERY** '91, Dry Creek Vly. $11.75
S	S	S		B				**SANTINO WINES** '89, Shenandoah Vly., Grandpere $12.00
B	G	S		S				**SEGHESIO WINERY** '91, Sonoma Co. $8.00
		S			Σ	S	S	**TRENTADUE** '90, Alexander Vly. $10.00
S		B		S		B		**VILLA MT. EDEN WINERY** '91, California, Cellar Select $10.00
								3 AWARDS
				B	G	B		**BARON HERZOG WINE CELLARS** '91, California $10.50
B		S		S				**BELVEDERE WINERY** '91, Dry Creek Vly. $10.00
	S		S		B			**BELVEDERE WINERY** '90, Dry Creek Vly. $10.00
	G			B	S			**GEYSER PEAK WINERY** '90, Dry Creek Vly. $9.00
B			S		B			**GREENWOOD RIDGE VINEYARDS** '91, Sonoma Co., Sherrer Vnyds. $12.50
B	B	B						**GUENOC WINERY** '90, California

Zinfandel	L.A. Orange Farmers	San Fran	Dallas	State Fair	New World	W. Coast	San Diego
3 AWARDS							
NAVARRO VINEYARDS '91, Mendocino $14.00		G		S		G	
PARDUCCI WINE CELLARS '90, Mendocino $7.00	S				S	G	
PERRY CREEK VINEYARDS '92, El Dorado Co. $8.00	G				S		G
QUIVIRA VINEYARDS '91, Dry Creek Vly. $13.25		B					S	B
RED ROCK WINERY '89, California $8.00		B	B				B
SANTA BARBARA WINERY '92, Santa Ynez Vly., Beaujour $9.00	S		S			G	
SANTINO WINES 'NV, Amador Co., Alfresco $6.00	S			B			S
SAUCELITO CANYON '91, Arroyo Grande Vly., Estate $12.00	G			S		Σ	
SEBASTIANI VINEYARDS '89, Sonoma Series $9.00				B	B		B
RODNEY STRONG VINEYARDS '90, River West, Old Vines Vnyd. $14.00		S			G	B	
SWANSON VINEYARDS '88, Napa Vly. $12.00			S		B		B
TOPOLOS AT RUSSIAN RIVER '91, Sonoma Co. $8.50		S				B	B
WHITE OAK VINEYARDS '91, Sonoma $9.00	S		S	S			
WINDSOR VINEYARDS '90, Alexander Vly., Reserve $12.00		B	S			S	
2 AWARDS							
BERINGER VINEYARDS '90, Napa Vly. $8.50	B			B			
DAVID BRUCE WINERY '91, SLO Co., Vintner's Select $12.50	B G						
BRUTOCAO CELLARS '91, Mendocino, Prop. Reserve $17.00			B				S
BYINGTON WINERY '90, Paso Robles, Sunny Slope Vnyd.						G	B
DAVIS BYNUM WINERY '91, Russian River Vly. $11.00	S			B			

112

L.A.	Orange Farmers	San Fran	Dallas	State Fair	New World	W. Coast	San Diego	Zinfandel
								2 AWARDS
				S		B		**CHATEAU SOUVERAIN** '91, Dry Creek Vly. $8.00
B			S					**CHESTNUT HILL** '90, California, Old Vines Cuvee $6.00
				B		B		**CLOS DU BOIS** '91, Sonoma $13.00
B			B					**DEER PARK WINERY** '89, Howell Mtn., Beatty Ranch Res.
				S		G		**FETZER VINEYARDS** '90, Mendocino Co., Reserve $12.50
		S		G				**J. FRITZ WINERY** '90, Dry Creek, 80 Year Old Vines $10.00
B				B				**GABRIELLI WINERY** '90, Mendocino Co. $10.00
				Σ		G		**GREEN & RED VINEYARD** '91, Napa Vly., Chiles Mill Vnyd. $13.00
				B	B			**GUNDLACH-BUNDSCHU** '91, Sonoma Vly. $10.00
		S		S				**HOP KILN WINERY** '90, Sonoma Co., Primitivo $15.00
B					B			**JANKRIS VINEYARD** '91, Paso Robles $8.50
	G		G					**KENDALL-JACKSON WINERY** '90, California, Vintner's Reserve
		S		B				**KENDALL-JACKSON WINERY** '90, Calif., Prop. Grand Reserve $20.00
				G	B			**KENDALL-JACKSON WINERY** '88, Mendocino, Ciapusci Vnyd. $20.00
	G			S				**KENWOOD VINEYARDS** '90, Sonoma Vly., Jack London $14.00
			B	B				**LATCHAM VINEYARDS** '90, El Dorado $8.00
			S		B			**LOUIS M. MARTINI WINERY** '89, Sonoma Co./Napa Co. $7.00
B				B				**NEVADA CITY WINERY** '91, Sierra Foothills $9.00
			B			B		**PRESTON VINEYARDS** '90, Dry Creek Vly.

Zinfandel	L.A.	Orange Farmers	San Fran	Dallas	State Fair	New World	W. Coast	San Diego
2 AWARDS								
RIVER RUN '92, California, LH $9.00	G				S			
ROSENBLUM CELLARS 'NV, California, Vintner's Cuvee VI $7.50	B		B					
ROSENBLUM CELLARS '91, Mt. Veeder, Brandlin Ranch $16.00			B	B				
ROSENBLUM CELLARS '91, Paso Robles, Richard Sauret $10.50	B					S		
ROSENBLUM CELLARS '91, Sonoma Co. $11.50					B			B
SANTINO WINES '89, Amador Co., White Harvest, LH $14.00		Σ						S
SANTINO WINES '89, Amador Co., Aged Release $8.00		B						S
V. SATTUI WINERY '90, Napa Vly., Suzanne's Vnyd. $12.75		B				G		
SONOMA CREEK WINERY '91, Sonoma Vly.						B		S
STORYBOOK MT. VINEYARDS '89, Napa Vly., Estate Reserve $19.50	B							B
STORYBOOK MT. VINEYARDS '88, Napa Vly., Reserve $19.50		B						S
TOPOLOS AT RUSSIAN RIVER '91, Sonoma Co., Rossi Ranch, Old Vines $14.50	S							B
WHITE OAK VINEYARDS '91, Sonoma Co., Ltd. Reserve $12.95	S				B			
WILD HORSE WINERY '90, Paso Robles			B		S			
WINDSOR VINEYARDS '90, Sonoma Co., Reserve $10.00	S		Σ					
WINDSOR VINEYARDS '90, Sonoma Co., Signature Series	B				B			

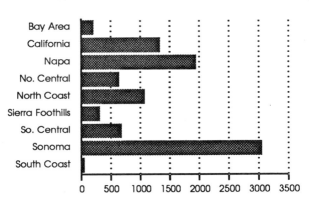

ALL VARIETALS

Regional Comparison of Total Points

(Gold-plus=7 Gold=5 Silver=3 Bronze=1)

Highest individual wine totals

238	**FETZER VINEYARDS** 13325 So. Highway 101, Hopland CA
198	**GEYSER PEAK WINERY** 22281 Chianti Rd., Geyserville CA 95441
188	**WINDSOR VINEYARDS** 11455 Old Redwood Hwy., Healdsburg CA
184	**BENZIGER WINERY** 1883 London Ranch Rd., Glen Ellen CA
183	**NAVARRO VINEYARDS** 5601 Highway 128, Philo CA 95466
167	**KENDALL-JACKSON WINERY** 640 Mathews Rd., Lakeport CA 95453
154	**MIRASSOU VINEYARDS** 3000 Aborn Rd., San Jose CA 95135
134	**GARY FARRELL WINES** P. O. Box 342, Forestville CA 95436
123	**BERINGER VINEYARDS** 2000 Main Street, St Helena CA 94574
113	**GUENOC WINERY** 21000 Butts Canyon Rd., Middletown CA
100	**CHATEAU ST. JEAN** 8555 Sonoma Hwy., Kenwood CA 95452
97	**HOP KILN WINERY** 6050 Westside Rd., Healdsburg CA 9544<n

89 VILLA MT. EDEN WINERY
620 Oakville Cross Rd., Oakville CA 94562

88 DE LOACH VINEYARDS
1791 Olivet Rd., Santa Rosa CA 95401

86 SEBASTIANI VINEYARDS
389 Fourth St. E., Sonoma CA 95476

85 HUSCH VINEYARDS
4400 Highway 128, Philo CA 95466

76 V. SATTUI WINERY
1111 White Lane, St Helena CA 94574

73 DRY CREEK VINEYARD
3770 Lambert Bridge, Healdsburg CA

70 COSENTINO WINERY
7415 St. Helena Hwy., Yountville CA

70 ESTANCIA WINERY
1178 Galleron Rd., Rutherford CA 94573

70 NAPA RIDGE
P. O. Box 111, St Helena CA 94574

69 GUNDLACH-BUNDSCHU
3775 Thornberry Road, Sonoma CA 95476

67 CHATEAU SOUVERAIN
400 Souverain Road, Geyserville CA 95441

66 HANDLEY CELLARS
P. O. Box 66, Philo CA 95466

65 GLORIA FERRER
23555 Highway 121, Sonoma CA 95476

65 MUMM CUVEE NAPA
1111 Dunaweal Ln., Calistoga CA 94515

61 WENTE BROS.
5565 Tesla Road, Livermore CA 94550

60 GLEN ELLEN WINERY
1883 London Ranch Rd., Glen Ellen CA

59 RABBIT RIDGE VINEYARDS
3291 Westside Rd., Healdsburg CA 95448

58 KENWOOD VINEYARDS
9592 Sonoma Highway, Kenwood CA

57 BELVEDERE WINERY
4035 Westside Road, Healdsburg CA

57 KORBEL
13250 River Rd., Forestville CA 95446

57 SANTINO WINES
Rt. 2, Box 21-A, Plymouth CA 95669

ABBEY D'OR
4620 Hog Canyon Rd. San Miguel 93451
Chardonnay,'91, Paso Robles (B-Dallas)

ACACIA
2750 Las Amigas Road Napa 94558
Chardonnay,'91, Napa, Carneros (2)
Pinot Noir,'90, Napa, Carneros, St. Clair $21.00 (2)
Pinot Noir,'91, Napa, Carneros (2)

ADELAIDA CELLARS
2170 Adelaida Rd. Paso Robles 93446
Cabernet Sauvignon,'89, Paso Robles $16.25 (5)
Cabernet Sauvignon,'90, San Luis Obispo $17.00 (4)
Chardonnay,'91, San Luis Obispo Co. $17.00 (4)

ADLER FELS WINERY
5325 Corrick Lane Santa Rosa 95405
Chardonnay,'90, Sonoma Co., Coleman Res. (S-State Fair)
Gewurztraminer,'92, Sonoma Co. $9.00 (6)
Sauvignon Blanc,'91, Sonoma Co., Fume $9.00 (2)
Sauvignon Blanc,'91, Sonoma Co., Organic $9.00 (S-San Diego)

AHLGREN VINEYARD
20320 Hwy. 9 Boulder Creek 95006
Cabernet Sauvignon,'89, Santa Cruz Mtns. (B-State Fair)

ALDERBROOK WINERY
2306 Magnolia Drive Healdsburg 95448
Chardonnay,'90, Dry Creek Vly. $11.00 (2)
Chardonnay,'90, Dry Creek Vly., Estate (S-San Diego)
Gewurztraminer,'92, Russian River Vly. $8.00 (3)
Sauvignon Blanc,'91, Dry Creek Vly., Estate $7.50 (4)
Semillon,'91, Dry Creek Vly. $9.00 (5)
White Meritage,'92, Dry Creek Vly., "Duet" $12.00 (3)

ALEXANDER VALLEY VINEYARDS
8644 Highway 128 Healdsburg 95448
Pinot Noir,'89, Alexander Vly., Estate (B-New World)

ALMADEN VINEYARDS
1530 Blossom Hill Rd. San Jose 95118
Johannisberg Riesling,'NV, California $2.49 (B-Orange)

ALPEN CELLARS
P.O. Box 3966 Trinity Center 96091
Gewurztraminer,'92, California $6.00 (B-Farmers)
Johannisberg Riesling,'92, Trinity Co. $6.00 (S-Orange)

AMADOR FOOTHILL WINERY
12500 Steiner Road Plymouth 95669
Sauvignon Blanc,'91, Shenandoah Vly., Fume $8.00 (2)

ANDERSON'S CONN VALLEY VINEYARD
680 Rossi St Helena 94574
Cabernet Sauvignon,'90, Napa Vly., Estate Reserve (S-Dallas)

S. ANDERSON VINEYARD
1473 Yountville Cross Rd. Yountville 94599
Chardonnay,'90, Napa Vly., Stag's Leap Dist. $18.00 (B-New World)

Chardonnay,'91, Stag's Leap Dist., Estate $18.00 (3)
Sparkling Wine,'87, Napa Vly., Brut $18.00 (8)
Sparkling Wine,'88, Napa Vly., Blanc de Noirs $20.00 (7)
Sparkling Wine,'89, Blanc De Noirs $20.00 (S-L.A.)

ANDRE
P.O. Box 1130 Modesto 95353
Sparkling Wine,'NV, California, Brut $2.79 (B-Orange)

ARCIERO WINERY
P. O. Box 1287 Paso Robles 93447
Cabernet Sauvignon,'89, Paso Robles (2)
Chardonnay,'91, Paso Robles, Estate $7.59 (3)
Chenin Blanc,'91, Paso Robles, Estate $4.29 (G-Orange)
Petite Sirah,'89, Paso Robles, Estate $7.50 (2)
Sauvignon Blanc,'90, Paso Robles, Estate $6.49 (S-Farmers)

ARMIDA WINERY
2201 Westside Road Healdsburg 95448
Chardonnay,'91, Russian River Vly. $10.00 (3)
Merlot,'90, Russian River Vly. $12.00 (3)
Pinot Noir,'91, Russian River Vly. (2)

ARROWOOD VINEYARDS
P. O. Box 987 Glen Ellen 95442
Cabernet Sauvignon,'89, Sonoma Co. $23.00 (S-Orange)
Merlot,'90, Sonoma Co. $27.00 (S-Orange)

VINCENT ARROYO WINERY
2361 Greenwood Ave. Calistoga 94515
Cabernet Sauvignon,'90, Napa Vly., Estate $18.00 (B-Farmers)

ASPEN GROVE
Address Not Available
Cabernet Sauvignon,'91, Sonoma Co., Reserve $9.00 (S-Orange)

AUDUBON CELLARS
600 Addison Street Berkeley 94710
Cabernet Sauvignon,'90, Napa Vly. $11.00 (2)
Cabernet Sauvignon,'91, Napa Vly., Oakville Ranch $11.00 (3)
Chardonnay,'91, Sonoma $9.00 (S-San Fran)
Sauvignon Blanc,'91, Napa Vly., Pope Vnyds. $9.00 (B-Orange)
Zinfandel,'91, Sonoma Co. (B-L.A.)

AUSTIN CELLARS
P. O. Box 636 Los Olivos 93441
Sauvignon Blanc,'91, Santa Barbara, Lucas Vnyd. $9.00 (3)

B

WILLIAM BACCALA ESTATE
4611 Thomas Road Healdsburg 95448
Chardonnay,'91, Sonoma $10.00 (2)
Merlot,'90, Napa Vly. (S-San Diego)

BAILEYANA
Address Not Available
Chardonnay,'91, Edna Vly., Paragon Vnyds. (3)

BAILY VINEYARD
36150 Pauba Road Temecula 92390
White Meritage,'91, Temecula, "Montage" (G-New World)

BALLATORE CHAMPAGNE
P. O. Box 1130 Modesto 95353
Sparkling Wine,'NV, California Gran Spumante $5.50 (6)

BANDIERA WINERY
155 Cherry Creek Rd. Cloverdale 95425
Cabernet Sauvignon,'89, Napa Vly. $7.00 (2)
White Zinfandel,'92, California (B-Dallas)

BANNISTER
Address Not Available
Chardonnay,'91, Russian River Vly. $15.00 (B-Orange)

BAREFOOT CELLARS
8075-B Westside Road Healdsburg 95448
Cabernet Sauvignon,'NV, California $4.00 (7)
Chardonnay,'NV, California $4.00 (2)
Sauvignon Blanc,'NV, California $4.00 (5)

BARGETTO WINERY
3535 N. Main Street Soquel 95073
Cabernet Sauvignon,'86, Santa Cruz Mtns. $18.00 (B-L.A.)
Cabernet Sauvignon,'90, Coastal Cellars $9.00 (B-L.A.)
Chardonnay,'90, Santa Cruz Mtns. $14.00 (2)
Gewurztraminer,'91, Monterey, Pinnacles Vnyd. $8.00 (B-Dallas)
Gewurztraminer,'92, Monterey Co. $8.00 (6)
Pinot Noir,'90, Santa Cruz, Sessantesimo $15.00 (2)
Sparkling Wine,'91, Santa Maria, Blanc De Noir $11.00 (2)

BARON HERZOG WINE CELLARS
12378 Saratoga-Sunnyvale Rd. Saratoga 95070
Cabernet Sauvignon,'91, California $12.00 (2)
Chardonnay,'91, California $10.75 (3)
Chenin Blanc,'92, California $5.95 (5)
Johannisberg Riesling,'91, Monterey Co., LH $7.95 (B-Dallas)
Johannisberg Riesling,'92, Monterey Co., LH $7.95 (G-Orange)
White Zinfandel,'92, California (4)
Zinfandel,'91, California $10.50 (3)

BEAU RIDGE
Address Not Available
Pinot Noir,'90, Santa Barbara Co. (S-Dallas)

BEAUCANON
1695 St. Helena Hwy. St Helena 94574
Cabernet Sauvignon,'88, Napa Vly. (S-State Fair)
Chardonnay,'91, Napa Vly., LH $10.00 (3)

BEAULIEU VINEYARD
1960 St. Helena Highway Rutherford 94573
Cabernet Sauvignon,'88, Napa Vly., Latour Reserve $37.00 (2)
Cabernet Sauvignon,'89, Napa Vly., Rutherford $13.00 (S-Dallas)
Cabernet Sauvignon,'90, Napa Vly., Beautour $9.00 (B-Orange)
Cabernet Sauvignon,'90, Napa Vly., Claret $8.00 (S-Orange)
Cabernet Sauvignon,'90, Napa Vly., Rutherford, Estate $13.00 (3)
Chardonnay,'89, Napa Vly., Carneros Reserve $17.00 (S-Dallas)
Chardonnay,'90, Napa Vly., Carneros Reserve $17.00 (2)
Chardonnay,'91, Napa Vly., Beautour $7.85 (2)
Pinot Noir,'90, Napa Vly. $9.00 (B-Dallas)
Pinot Noir,'90, Napa, Carneros Reserve $17.00 (4)

Pinot Noir,'91, Napa Vly. $9.00 (S-L.A.)
Sauvignon Blanc,'91, Napa Vly., Fume, Beautour $7.75 (B-Orange)

BEL ARBORS

13325 So. Highway 101 Hopland 95449

Cabernet Sauvignon,'90, California, Founder's Sel. $6.75 (4)
Chardonnay,'92, California, Founder's Sel. $7.00 (5)
Merlot,'91, California, Founder's Sel $7.00 (4)
Sauvignon Blanc,'92, California, Founder's Sel. $5.00 (S-Orange)
White Zinfandel,'92, California, Founder's Sel. $5.00 (5)
Zinfandel,'90, California (B-New World)

BELVEDERE WINERY

4035 Westside Road Healdsburg 95448

Chardonnay,'90, Russian River Vly. $13.00 (3)
Chardonnay,'90, Sonoma Co. $18.00 (2)
Chardonnay,'91, Alexander Vly. $9.00 (3)
Chardonnay,'91, Russian River Vly. $13.00 (S-State Fair)
Chardonnay,'91, Sonoma, Preferred Stock $18.00 (4)
Merlot,'90, Dry Creek Vly. $14.00 (3)
Zinfandel,'90, Dry Creek Vly. $10.00 (3)
Zinfandel,'91, Dry Creek Vly. $10.00 (3)

BENZIGER WINERY

1883 London Ranch Rd. Glen Ellen 95442

Cabernet Sauvignon,'88, Sonoma Mtn. (G-New World)
Cabernet Sauvignon,'89, Sonoma Mtn., Estate $21.75 (B-Orange)
Cabernet Sauvignon,'90, Sonoma Co. $12.50 (6)
Chardonnay,'91, Carneros $16.00 (2)
Chardonnay,'91, Sonoma Co. $12.50 (6)
Merlot,'89, Sonoma Mtn. (B-New World)
Merlot,'90, Sonoma Co. $14.00 (6)
Petite Sirah,'89, California (B-W. Coast)
Pinot Blanc,'91, Sonoma Co. $10.00 (6)
Pinot Noir,'90, Sonoma Co. $12.50 (4)
Red Meritage,'89, Sonoma Mtn. "A Tribute" $27.00 (6)
Sauvignon Blanc,'91, Sonoma Co., Fume $9.00 (2)
Sauvignon Blanc,'91, Sonoma Mtn., Estate $13.50 (3)
Sauvignon Blanc,'92, Sonoma Co. $9.00 (B-L.A.)
Semillon,'90, Sonoma Mtn. Estate $13.50 (2)
Semillon,'91, Sonoma Mtn., Estate $13.50 (S-L.A.)
Sparkling Wine,'88, Sonoma, Blanc de Blancs $12.00 (3)
White Meritage,'90, Sonoma Mtn., "A Tribute" $15.00 (3)
White Meritage,'91, Sonoma Mtn., "A Tribute" $15.00 (B-L.A.)
Zinfandel,'90, Sonoma Co. $10.00 (4)

BERGFELD WINERY

401 St. Helena Hwy., So. St Helena 94574

Cabernet Franc,'89, Napa Vly., Estate $11.00 (S-Farmers)
Cabernet Sauvignon,'91, Napa Vly. $7.00 (G-San Fran)
Chardonnay,'91, Napa Vly., Estate $11.00 (2)
Merlot,'89, Napa Vly., Estate (3)
Merlot,'90, Napa Vly. (2)

BERINGER VINEYARDS

2000 Main Street St Helena 94574

Cabernet Sauvignon,'87, Napa Vly., Chabot Vnyd. $32.00 (3)
Cabernet Sauvignon,'88, Napa Vly., Chabot Vnyd. $35.00 (2)
Cabernet Sauvignon,'88, Napa Vly., Reserve $45.00 (B-San Diego)

Cabernet Sauvignon,'89, Napa Vly. (B-L.A.)
Cabernet Sauvignon,'89, Napa Vly., Reserve $45.00 (2)
Chardonnay,'91, Napa Vly., Proprieter Grown (S-State Fair)
Chardonnay,'91, Napa Vly., Reserve $19.00 (4)
Chardonnay,'91, Napa Vly., Sbragia (2)
Chenin Blanc,'91, Napa Vly. $8.00 (B-San Fran)
Chenin Blanc,'92, Napa Vly., Beringer Vnyds. $7.50 (2)
Gewurztraminer,'91, North Coast $7.50 (B-Dallas)
Gewurztraminer,'92, California, Prop. Grown $7.50 (2)
Johannisberg Riesling,'91, North Coast $8.00 (3)
Johannisberg Riesling,'92, California, Beringer Vnyds. $7.50 (2)
Merlot,'89, Howell Mtn., Bancroft Ranch $28.50 (2)
Merlot,'90, Howell Mtn., Bancroft Ranch $28.50 (S-L.A.)
Sauvignon Blanc,'90, Napa Vly., Fume $9.00 (B-San Fran)
Sauvignon Blanc,'91, Napa Vly., Fume $9.00 (3)
White Meritage,'91, Knights Vly. $9.00 (8)
White Zinfandel,'92, North Coast $6.00 (4)
Zinfandel,'89, Napa Co. $8.50 (7)
Zinfandel,'90, Napa Vly. $8.50 (2)

BERNARDUS
Address Not Available
Chardonnay,'91, California (B-State Fair)
Sauvignon Blanc,'91, Monterey Co. (B-Dallas)
Sauvignon Blanc,'92, Monterey Co. $8.00 (B-Orange)

BETTINELLI
Address Not Available
Chardonnay,'90, Napa Vly. $9.00 (B-Orange)

BIANCHI VINEYARDS
5806 N. Modoc Ave. Kerman 93630
Chardonnay,'92, California, Reserve (B-San Diego)

BLACK MOUNTAIN VINEYARD
101 Grant Ave. Healdsburg 95448
Cabernet Sauvignon,'90, Alexander Vly., Fat Cat $18.00 (2)
Petite Sirah,'90, Alexander Vly., Bosun Crest $10.00 (2)

BLOSSOM HILL COLLECTION
P. O. Box 391 St Helena 94574
Johannisberg Riesling,'NV, California, Reserve $3.75 (S-Orange)

BOEGER WINERY
1709 Carson Road Placerville 95667
Cabernet Sauvignon,'89, El Dorado (2)
Red Meritage,'89, El Dorado (S-State Fair)
Sauvignon Blanc,'91, El Dorado, Estate $7.50 (2)
Zinfandel,'91, El Dorado, Walker $10.00 (B-San Fran)

BOGLE VINEYARDS
Rt. 1, Box 276 Clarksburg 95612
Cabernet Sauvignon,'91, California $6.50 (S-Orange)
Chardonnay,'92, California $6.50 (B-State Fair)
Chardonnay,'92, California, Reserve $12.00 (B-State Fair)
Chenin Blanc,'92, Clarksburg (S-State Fair)
Merlot,'91, California $8.00 (3)
Petite Sirah,'91, California $6.00 (S-New World)
White Zinfandel,'92, California $5.00 (B-Orange)

BON MARCHE
820 Greenfield Rd. St Helena 94574
Cabernet Sauvignon,'91, Sonoma Co. $8.00 (4)
Chardonnay,'91, Sonoma Co. $8.00 (B-San Diego)

BOYER WINERY
P. O. Box 842 Soledad 93960
Chardonnay,'91, Monterey Co., Ventana Vnyd. $13.00 (B-Orange)

BRANDER VINEYARD
P. O. Box 92 Los Olivos 93441
Chardonnay,'91, Tete de Cuvee $16.00 (S-San Fran)
Red Meritage,'89, Santa Ynez Vly., Bouchet $20.00 (S-Farmers)
Red Meritage,'90, Santa Ynez Vly., Bouchet $18.00 (B-San Fran)
Sauvignon Blanc,'91, Santa Ynez Vly. $9.75 (2)
White Meritage,'91, Tete De Cuvee (Σ-L.A.)

BRAREN PAULI WINERY
1613 Spring Hill Rd Petaluma 94952
Cabernet Sauvignon,'89, Dry Creek Vly., Mauritson Vnyd. $13.00 (2)
Cabernet Sauvignon,'90, Dry Creek Vly. $13.00 (4)

BRIARWOOD CELLARS
14653 Titus St. Panorama City 91402
Chardonnay,'91, California (B-New World)
Sauvignon Blanc,'92, California (G-New World)

BRICELAND VINEYARDS
5959 Briceland Rd. Redway 95560
Sauvignon Blanc,'92, Humboldt Co. $9.50 (2)
Sparkling Wine,'NV, Brut, Humboldt Co. (G-State Fair)

DAVID BRUCE WINERY
21439 Bear Creek Rd. Los Gatos 95030
Cabernet Sauvignon,'90, Mendocino, Reserve, Select $18.00 (4)
Chardonnay,'90, Santa Cruz Mtns., Reserve $30.00 (2)
Chardonnay,'91, Santa Cruz Mtns., Reserve $30.00 (G-Orange)
Chardonnay,'91, Santa Cruz Mtns.,Barrel Ferm. $18.00 (S-L.A.)
Chardonnay,'91, Santa Cruz, Meyley Vnyd. $18.00 (2)
Petite Sirah,'91, California, Vintner's Select $12.50 (3)
Pinot Noir,'90, California, Vintner's Select $12.50 (2)
Pinot Noir,'90, Santa Cruz Mtns., Estate (2)
Pinot Noir,'90, Santa Cruz Mtns., Reserve $30.00 (4)
Pinot Noir,'91, Russian River Valley Reserve (S-State Fair)
Zinfandel,'91, SLO Co., Vintner's Select $12.50 (2)

RUTOCAO CELLARS
P.O. Box 780 Hopland 95449
Cabernet Sauvignon,'88, Mendocino Co. (B-State Fair)
Merlot,'91, Mendocino Co. $15.00 (8)
Sauvignon Blanc,'91, Mendocino Co. $8.50 (S-Orange)
Sauvignon Blanc,'92, Mendocino $8.50 (S-New World)
Zinfandel,'91, Mendocino, Prop. Reserve $17.00 (2)

UEHLER VINEYARDS
820 Greenfield Rd. St Helena 94574
White Zinfandel,'92, Napa Vly. (S-San Diego)

BUENA VISTA WINERY

27000 Ramal Road Sonoma 95476

Cabernet Sauvignon,'88, Carneros $12.00 (B-W. Coast)
Cabernet Sauvignon,'89, Carneros, Grand Reserve (B-New World)
Cabernet Sauvignon,'90, Carneros $11.00 (2)
Chardonnay,'91, Carneros $11.00 (4)
Merlot,'89, Carneros, Grand Reserve $18.00 (G-New World)
Pinot Noir,'91, Carneros $10.00 (B-Orange)
Sauvignon Blanc,'91, Lake Co. $7.50 (4)
Sauvignon Blanc,'92, Lake Co. $7.50 (4)

BURGESS CELLARS

1108 Deer Park Rd. St Helena 94574

Cabernet Sauvignon,'89, Napa Vly. $18.00 (4)
Chardonnay,'91, Napa Vly., Triere Vnyd. (S-L.A.)
Zinfandel,'90, Napa Vly. $10.00 (4)

BUTTERFLY CREEK WINERY

4063 Bear Creek Road Mariposa 95338

Chardonnay,'91, California (B-State Fair)
Pinot Blanc,'91, California, LH $7.25 (B-Farmers)

BYINGTON WINERY

21850 Bear Creek Rd. Los Gatos 95030

Sauvignon Blanc,'91, Livermore Vly., Fume (B-New World)
Zinfandel,'90, Paso Robles, Sunny Slope Vnyd. (2)

DAVIS BYNUM WINERY

8075 Westside Rd. Healdsburg 95448

Chardonnay,'91, Russian Riv., Allen-Griffin Vnyds. $17.00 (4)
Chardonnay,'92, Russian River Vly. $10.00 (B-Farmers)
Gewurztraminer,'91, Russian River Vly. $8.00 (B-Dallas)
Gewurztraminer,'92, Russian River Vly. $8.00 (4)
Merlot,'91, Sonoma Co., Ltd. Release $13.00 (2)
Pinot Noir,'90, Russian River Vly., Ltd. Release $18.00 (3)
Pinot Noir,'91, Russian River Vly. $12.00 (2)
Sauvignon Blanc,'92, Russian Riv., Shone Farm, Fume $8.50 (4)
Zinfandel,'91, Russian River Vly. $11.00 (2)

BYRON VINEYARD

5230 Tepusquet Rd. Santa Maria 93454

Chardonnay,'91, Santa Barbara Co. $14.00 (3)
Chardonnay,'91, Santa Barbara Co., Reserve $20.00 (4)
Pinot Blanc,'92, Santa Barbara Co. (S-L.A.)
Pinot Noir,'90, Santa Barbara Co. (B-Dallas)
Pinot Noir,'91, Santa Barbara Co., Reserve $22.50 (S-Orange)
Pinot Noir,'91, Santa Barbara Co., Reserve (S-State Fair)
Sauvignon Blanc,'92, Santa Barbara Co. (S-San Diego)

C

CAIN CELLARS

3800 Langtry Rd. St Helena 94574

Red Meritage,'87, Napa Vly. $18.79 (B-Orange)
Red Meritage,'88, Napa Vly., Cuvee (2)
Red Meritage,'89, Napa Vly. Cuvee (G-State Fair)
Sauvignon Blanc,'91, Monterey, Musque $12.00 (B-San Fran)

CAKEBREAD CELLARS
8300 St. Helena Hwy. Rutherford 94573
Cabernet Sauvignon,'90, Napa Vly. $21.00 (B-Orange)
Chardonnay,'91, Napa Vly. $20.00 (B-Orange)

CALE CELLARS
2501 Barona Pl. Santa Rosa 95405
Chardonnay,'91, Carneros, Sangiacomo Vnyd. $18.00 (2)

CALLAWAY VINEYARD
32720 Rancho California Temecula 92390
Cabernet Sauvignon,'90, California $10.00 (4)
Johannisberg Riesling,'92, Temecula $7.00 (2)
Sauvignon Blanc,'91, Temecula, Fume $8.00 (3)
Sparkling Wine,'88, Temecula, Blanc de Blanc $16.00 (2)

CAMBRIA WINERY
Route 1, Box 142 Santa Maria 93454
Chardonnay,'89, Santa Maria Vly., Reserve $25.00 (G-New World)
Chardonnay,'90, Santa Maria Vly., Reserve $25.00 (6)
Chardonnay,'91, Santa Maria, Katherine's Vnyd. $16.00 (4)
Pinot Noir,'91, Santa Maria Vly., Julia's Vnyd. $16.00 (S-State Fair)

CANEPA CELLARS
Address Not Available
Chardonnay,'91, Alexander Vly., Canepa Vnyd. $17.00 (B-Orange)

CANYON ROAD CELLARS
22281 Chianti Rd. Geyserville 95441
Cabernet Sauvignon,'91, California $4.75 (4)
Chardonnay,'92, California $4.75 (4)
Sauvignon Blanc,'92, California $4.75 (5)

CAREY CELLARS
1711 Alamo Pintado Rd. Solvang 93463
Sauvignon Blanc,'91, Santa Ynez Vly. $8.00 (2)

CARMENET
1700 Moon Mountain Rd Sonoma 95476
Cabernet Franc,'90, Sonoma Vly. $20.00 (S-Orange)
Cabernet Sauvignon,'91, Sonoma Vly., Dynamite $15.00 (2)
Red Meritage,'87, Sonoma Vly., Red Table Wine (B-New World)
Red Meritage,'89, Sonoma Vly., Moon Mtn. $21.50 (B-Orange)

CARNEROS CREEK WINERY
1285 Dealy Lane Napa 94559
Chardonnay,'91, Carneros, Dry $14.00 (S-San Fran)
Pinot Noir,'91, Fleur de Carneros $10.00 (3)

MAURICE CARRIE WINERY
34225 Rancho Calif. Rd. Temecula 92390
Chardonnay,'90, Temecula (B-New World)
Chardonnay,'91, Temecula Vly., Reserve $9.00 (3)
Chenin Blanc,'91, Temecula, Soft $4.00 (3)
Merlot,'91, California $8.00 (5)
Pinot Noir,'90, Santa Barbara Co. $12.00 (B-Dallas)
Sauvignon Blanc,'91, Temecula $5.00 (2)

CASTORO CELLARS
1480 No. Bethel Road Templeton 93465
Cabernet Sauvignon,'90, Paso Robles $10.00 (2)

Cabernet Sauvignon,'90, Paso Robles, Reserve $13.00 (2)
Chardonnay,'92, San Luis Obispo Co. $9.50 (5)
Pinot Noir,'91, Santa Barbara Co. $10.50 (B-Orange)
Sauvignon Blanc,'92, San Luis Obispo (B-W. Coast)
White Zinfandel,'92, San Luis Obispo $6.00 (4)
Zinfandel,'90, Paso Robles $9.00 (5)

CAYMUS VINEYARDS
8700 Conn Creek Road   Rutherford   94573
Cabernet Sauvignon,'89, Napa Vly. $24.00 (2)
Cabernet Sauvignon,'90, California, Vintner Select (2)
Cabernet Sauvignon,'91, Paso Robles, Liberty School (B-L.A.)
Zinfandel,'91, Napa Vly. $10.00 (B-San Fran)

CEDAR MOUNTAIN WINERY
7000 Tesla Road   Livermore   94550
Cabernet Sauvignon,'90, Livermore, Blanches $20.00 (S-San Fran)

CHALK HILL WINERY
10300 Chalk Hill Rd.   Healdsburg   95448
Cabernet Sauvignon,'90, Chalk Hill, Estate (2)
Chardonnay,'90, Sonoma, Estate $17.00 (S-San Fran)
Chardonnay,'91, Sonoma Co., Chalk Hill $17.00 (3)
Sauvignon Blanc,'91, Sonoma Co., Estate $10.00 (2)

CHALONE VINEYARD
P.O. Box 855   Soledad   93960
Pinot Noir,'90, Chalone, Estate (S-New World)

CHANSA CELLARS
P. O. Box 2375   Santa Maria   93455
Pinot Noir,'90, Santa Barbara Co. (S-New World)

CHAPPELLET VINEYARD
1581 Sage Canyon Rd   St Helena   94574
Cabernet Sauvignon,'90, Napa Vly., Signature $25.00 (B-San Fran)
Chardonnay,'90, Napa Vly. $14.00 (S-Dallas)
Chenin Blanc,'91, Napa Vly. $8.00 (B-San Fran)

CHASE LIMOGERE
P. O. Box 55   Woodbridge   95258
Sparkling Wine,'NV, California Brut $6.00 (B-Dallas)

CHATEAU DE BAUN WINERY
5007 Fulton Road   Fulton   95439
Chardonnay,'91, Russian River Vly. $10.00 (5)
Pinot Noir,'90, Sonoma Co. $6.00 (B-San Diego)
Sparkling Wine,'NV, Sonoma Co. Brut $12.00 (2)
Sparkling Wine,'NV, Sonoma Co. Brut Rose $12.00 (2)

CHATEAU DE LEU WINERY
1635 W. Mason Rd   Suisun   94585
Cabernet Sauvignon,'89, Napa Vly. $14.00 (S-New World)
Chardonnay,'90, Napa Vly. $11.00 (3)
Chardonnay,'91, Solano Co., Green Vly. $14.00 (B-State Fair)
Merlot,'91, Napa Vly. $12.00 (B-W. Coast)
Pinot Noir,'90, Napa Vly. $12.00 (2)
Red Meritage,'91, North Coast (S-W. Coast)

CHATEAU JULIEN WINERY
8940 Carmel Valley Rd. Carmel 93923
Cabernet Sauvignon,'89, Monterey Co., Reserve $13.00 (2)
Chardonnay,'91, Monterey Co., Surlie, Reserve $13.00 (2)
Chardonnay,'92, Monterey Co., Barrel Ferm. (B-State Fair)
Merlot,'91, Monterey Co. $14.00 (B-San Diego)

CHATEAU POMIJE WINERY
Address Not Available
Chardonnay,'92, San Luis Obispo (B-San Diego)
Chardonnay,'92, San Luis Obispo, Ivy Hills, Reserve (S-San Diego)
Chardonnay,'92, San Luis Obispo, Ruby, Reserve (B-San Diego)
White Zinfandel,'92, SLO Co., Ruby, Reserve (B-San Diego)

CHATEAU SOUVERAIN
400 Souverain Road Geyserville 95441
Cabernet Sauvignon,'88, Alexander Vly., Reserve $13.00 (3)
Cabernet Sauvignon,'89, Alexander Vly. $10.50 (3)
Cabernet Sauvignon,'90, Alexander Vly. $11.00 (2)
Chardonnay,'90, Sangiacomo, Res. $14.00 (B-New World)
Chardonnay,'91, Sonoma Co., Barrel Ferm. $10.00 (3)
Merlot,'90, Alexander Vly. $10.50 (5)
Merlot,'90, Sonoma Co. $10.50 (G-New World)
Merlot,'91, Alexander Vly. $10.50 (3)
Pinot Noir,'91, Carneros, Reserve $13.50 (2)
Sauvignon Blanc,'91, Alexander Vly., Barrel Ferm. $7.50 (S-Orange)
Sauvignon Blanc,'92, Alexander Vly. $7.50 (B-State Fair)
Zinfandel,'90, Dry Creek Vly. $8.00 (4)
Zinfandel,'91, Dry Creek Vly. $8.00 (2)

CHATEAU ST. JEAN
8555 Sonoma Hwy. Kenwood 95452
Cabernet Sauvignon,'88, Sonoma Co., Reserve $80.00 (B-Orange)
Cabernet Sauvignon,'89, Sonoma Co. $18.00 (9)
Chardonnay,'90, Alexander Vly., Belle Terre $17.50 (B-Farmers)
Chardonnay,'90, Robt. Young Vnyd., Reserve $41.95 (B-Farmers)
Chardonnay,'91, Sonoma Co. (S-New World)
Gewurztraminer,'91, Frank Johnson, SLH $15.00 (3)
Johannisberg Riesling,'89, Hoot Owl Creek, SSLH $20.00 (5)
Johannisberg Riesling,'91, Sonoma Co. $9.00 (B-New World)
Merlot,'89, Sonoma Co. $17.00 (3)
Pinot Noir,'90, Sonoma Co. (B-W. Coast)
Sauvignon Blanc,'91, Russian River, Fume $11.00 (2)
Sparkling Wine,'85, Grande Cuvee $20.00 (S-L.A.)
Sparkling Wine,'NV, Sonoma Co. Brut $12.00 (4)
Sparkling Wine,'NV, Sonoma, Blanc de Blanc $12.00 (7)

CHATEAU THOMAS
Address Not Available
Cabernet Sauvignon,'87, Napa, Hornerberger (B-San Diego)
Pinot Noir,'89, Los Carneros (B-San Diego)

CHATOM VINEYARDS
7449 Esmeralda Rd San Andreas 95249
Cabernet Sauvignon,'89, Calaveras Co. (S-State Fair)
Cabernet Sauvignon,'90, Calaveras Co. $14.00 (2)

CHAUFEE-EAU CELLARS
24401 Chianti Road Geyserville 95441
Chardonnay,'91, Carneros, Sangiacomo $16.00 (3)

CHESTNUT HILL
75 Broadway, #207 San Francisco 94111
Cabernet Sauvignon,'90, California, Coastal Cuvee (2)
Merlot,'91, North Coast, Coastal Cuvee $10.50 (4)
Zinfandel,'90, California, Old Vines Cuvee $6.00 (2)

CHEVAL SAUVAGE
P. O. Box 638 Templeton 93465
Merlot,'90, Paso Robles $29.95 (B-Orange)
Pinot Noir,'90, Paso Robles $28.00 (2)
Pinot Noir,'90, Santa Barbara $28.00 (S-San Fran)

CHIMERE WINERY
547 W. Betteravia #D Santa Maria 93454
Chardonnay,'91, Santa Barbara Co. (S-Dallas)

CHIMNEY ROCK
5320 Silverado Trail Napa 94558
Cabernet Sauvignon,'89, Napa Vly., Stag's Leap Dist. $18.00 (2)

CHOUINARD VINEYARDS
33853 Palomares Rd. Castro Valley 94552
Petite Sirah,'91, Napa Vly. $11.00 (2)

CHRISTIAN BROTHERS
P. O. Box 391 St Helena 94574
Chardonnay,'91, Napa Vly. $6.00 (G-Orange)
White Zinfandel,'92, California $3.00 (B-Orange)

CHRISTOPHER CREEK
641 Limerick Lane Healdsburg 95448
Petite Sirah,'89, Russian River Vly., Estate $13.00 (B-New World)
Petite Sirah,'90, Russian River Vly. $13.00 (6)
Syrah,'90, Russian River Vly., Estate $14.00 (7)

CILURZO VINEYARD
41220 Calle Contento Temecula 92390
Merlot,'90, Temecula, Prop. Reserve $12.00 (S-Orange)
Petite Sirah,'90, Temecula, Prop. Reserve $12.00 (2)
Petite Sirah,'92, Temecula, Nouveau $7.00 (B-State Fair)
Sauvignon Blanc,'92, Temecula, Luiseno Vnyd. (S-San Diego)
White Zinfandel,'91, Temecula $4.95 (B-Farmers)

CINNABAR
23000 Congress Springs Rd. Saratoga 95071
Chardonnay,'90, Santa Cruz Mtns. $20.00 (3)

CLAIBORNE & CHURCHILL
860 Capitolio Way San Luis Obispo 93406
Gewurztraminer,'91, Central Coast (B-San Diego)

CLAUDIA SPRINGS WINERY
2160 Guntly Road Philo 95466
Pinot Noir,'91, Anderson Vly. $12.50 (2)

CLIMARA
Address Not Available
Semillon,'86, Central Coast, Botrytis $30.00 (2)

CLINE CELLARS
24737 Arnold Drive Sonoma 95476
Semillon,'91, California, Barrel Ferm. (3)
Syrah,'91, Contra Costa Co. $14.50 (4)
Zinfandel,'91, Contra Costa Co. $9.00 (5)

CLONINGER CELLARS
Address Not Available
Cabernet Sauvignon,'90, Monterey Co. $15.00 (2)
Chardonnay,'88, Monterey $15.00 (S-New World)
Chardonnay,'89, Monterey Co. $15.00 (S-San Diego)
Chardonnay,'91, Monterey $15.00 (B-San Fran)

CLOS DU BOIS
5 Fitch Street Healdsburg 95448
Cabernet Sauvignon,'89, Alexander Vly. $12.75 (B-W. Coast)
Cabernet Sauvignon,'89, Briarcrest $21.00 (S-New World)
Cabernet Sauvignon,'90, Alexander Vly. $12.75 (3)
Chardonnay,'90, Dry Creek Vly. (G-W. Coast)
Chardonnay,'90, Dry Creek Vly., Flintwood $17.00 (B-New World)
Chardonnay,'91, Alexander Vly. (3)
Chardonnay,'91, Alexander Vly., Calcaire $18.50 (B-State Fair)
Chardonnay,'91, Dry Creek Vly., Flintwood $17.00 (B-San Diego)
Merlot,'89, Alexander Vly., Reserve (S-San Diego)
Merlot,'90, Sonoma Co. $15.00 (4)
Pinot Noir,'90, Sonoma Co. (B-State Fair)
Red Meritage,'89, Alexander Vly. $20.00 (B-W. Coast)
Sauvignon Blanc,'92, Alexander Vly., Barrel Ferm. $8.00 (4)
Zinfandel,'91, Sonoma $13.00 (2)

CLOS DU VAL
5330 Silverado Trail Napa 94558
Cabernet Sauvignon,'87, Stags Leap Dist. $18.00 (B-New World)
Cabernet Sauvignon,'89, Napa Vly., Stags Leap Dist. $18.00 (3)
Chardonnay,'91, Napa Vly., Carneros $14.00 (3)
Red Meritage,'88, Napa Vly., Reserve $48.00 (S-Orange)
Semillon,'89, Stags Leap Dist. $10.00 (B-San Fran)

CLOS PEGASE WINERY
1060 Dunaweal Ln. Calistoga 94515
Cabernet Sauvignon,'89, Napa Vly. $16.50 (S-Farmers)
Chardonnay,'90, Napa Vly. $13.00 (3)
Merlot,'90, Napa Vly. $15.50 (2)

LOS ROBERT
Address Not Available
Merlot,'91, Napa Vly. $7.00 (B-Orange)

COASTAL CELLARS
Address Not Available
Chardonnay,'91, California $5.00 (G-Orange)
Sauvignon Blanc,'91, California $4.00 (B-Orange)

R. COHN
P.O. Box 1673 Sonoma 95476
Cabernet Sauvignon,'89, Sonoma Vly. (B-W. Coast)

CONCANNON VINEYARD
4590 Tesla Road Livermore 94550
Chardonnay,'91, Mistral/Kalthof/Hayes Vnyds. (B-State Fair)

Johannisberg Riesling,'92, Anderson Vly., LH $8.95 (2)
Johannisberg Riesling,'92, Arroyo Seco., Selected Vnyds. $8.00 (4)
Petite Sirah,'90, Livermore Vly., Reserve $14.95 (B-Farmers)
Semillon,'92, Livermore Vly., Estate (2)
White Meritage,'91, Livermore Vly., Assemblage $14.95 (2)

CONN CREEK WINERY
8711 Silverado Trail St Helena 94574
Cabernet Sauvignon,'88, Napa Vly., Barrel Sel. $16.00 (7)
Cabernet Sauvignon,'89, Napa Vly., Reserve $23.00 (6)
Chardonnay,'91, California, Cellar Select (S-State Fair)
Chardonnay,'91, Napa, Carneros, Grand Res. (S-State Fair)
Merlot,'89, Napa Vly., Barrel Select (3)
Merlot,'90, Napa Vly., Grand Reserve (S-State Fair)
Zinfandel,'91, California, Cellar Select (B-State Fair)

COOK'S CHAMPAGNE CELLARS
391 Taylor Blvd., #110 Pleasant Hill 94523
Chardonnay,'91, California, Reserve (2)
Merlot,'91, California, Captain's Reserve $6.00 (4)
Sparkling Wine,'NV, American Spumante $3.99 (5)
Sparkling Wine,'NV, American, Grand Reserve $3.99 (2)
Sparkling Wine,'NV, American, Imperial, Blush $3.99 (3)
Sparkling Wine,'NV, American, Imperial, Brut $3.99 (2)
Sparkling Wine,'NV, American, Imperial, Extra Dry $3.99 (2)
Sparkling Wine,'NV, American, Imperial, White Zin. $3.99 (B-Orange)
White Zinfandel,'92, California, Reserve $3.99 (B-State Fair)

CORBETT CANYON VINEYARDS
2195 Corbett Canyon Rd. San Luis Obispo 93406
Cabernet Sauvignon,'90, Calif., Coastal Classic $8.00 (B-Dallas)
Cabernet Sauvignon,'90, Napa Vly., Reserve $9.00 (B-State Fair)
Cabernet Sauvignon,'91, California, Coastal Classic $8.00 (3)
Chardonnay,'91, Central Coast, Coastal Classic $8.00 (2)
Chardonnay,'91, Santa Barbara Co., Reserve $9.00 (B-Farmers)
Merlot,'91, California Coastal Classic $7.00 (4)
Pinot Noir,'91, Santa Barbara Co., Reserve $9.00 (S-State Fair)
Sauvignon Blanc,'92, Central Coast, Coastal Classic $4.50 (6)

CORDONIU NAPA
1345 Henry Road Napa 94558
Sparkling Wine,'NV, Napa Vly. Brut $15.00 (3)

CORISON
Address Not Available
Cabernet Sauvignon,'89, Napa Vly. $25.00 (B-Orange)

COSENTINO WINERY
7415 St. Helena Hwy. Yountville 94599
Cabernet Franc,'90, North Coast $16.00 (3)
Cabernet Franc,'91, North Coast $18.00 (3)
Cabernet Sauvignon,'88, North Coast, Reserve $25.00 (2)
Cabernet Sauvignon,'90, Napa Vly. $16.00 (3)
Chardonnay,'91, Napa Vly. $14.00 (2)
Chardonnay,'91, Napa Vly., The Sculptor $20.00 (4)
Merlot,'90, Napa Vly. $18.00 (3)
Merlot,'91, Napa Vly. $18.00 (G-Orange)
Pinot Noir,'91, Carneros $18.00 (2)
Red Meritage,'90, California, "The Poet" $25.00 (3)

White Meritage,'92, Napa Vly., "The Novelist" (S-State Fair)
Zinfandel,'91, Sonoma Co., "The Zin" (G-L.A.)

COTES DE SONOMA
P. O. Box 2386 So San Francisco 94083
Chardonnay,'92, Sonoma Co. $7.00 (B-Orange)
Sauvignon Blanc,'92, Sonoma Co. $6.00 (2)

THOMAS COYNE WINES
2162 Broadmoor St. Livermore 94550
Merlot,'90, Sonoma Co. (S-New World)
Petite Sirah,'90, Napa Vly./El Dorado $10.00 (B-Orange)
Red Meritage,'90, Napa Vly., "Cabernets" (2)

M. COZ
7415 St. Helena Hwy. Yountville 94599
Red Meritage,'90, Napa Vly. $45.00 (2)

CRESTON VINEYARDS
679 Calf Canyon Hwy. Creston 93432
Cabernet Sauvignon,'89, Paso Robles $10.00 (6)
Cabernet Sauvignon,'89, Paso Robles, Winemakers Sel. $17.00 (2)
Merlot,'90, Paso Robles $13.00 (3)
Pinot Noir,'91, Paso Robles $9.00 (2)
Sauvignon Blanc,'90, Paso Robles, Estate $8.25 (S-Farmers)
Semillon,'92, Paso Robles, Chevier Blanc $9.00 (B-Farmers)
White Meritage,'92, Paso Robles, Estate $9.00 (B-Orange)
White Zinfandel,'92, Paso Robles $6.00 (3)

CRICHTON HALL
P. O. Box 9008 Rutherford 94573
Chardonnay,'91, Napa, Chardonnay Vnyd. $18.00 (6)

CULBERTSON WINERY
32575 Rancho Calif. Rd. Temecula 92591
Sparkling Wine,'84, Founders Reserve (B-L.A.)
Sparkling Wine,'86, California, Blanc de Blancs $20.00 (B-San Fran)
Sparkling Wine,'87, California, Brut $16.00 (2)
Sparkling Wine,'87, California, Brut Rose (2)
Sparkling Wine,'87, California, Natural $16.00 (2)
Sparkling Wine,'NV, Calif., Cuvee de Frontignan $12.00 (3)
Sparkling Wine,'NV, California Brut $10.00 (B-Farmers)
Sparkling Wine,'NV, California, Cuvee Rouge $12.00 (2)

RICHARD CUNEO
389 Fourth St. E. Sonoma 95476
Sparkling Wine,'88, Sonoma, Blanc de Blanc $14.00 (2)

CUVAISON
P. O. Box 2230 Napa 94559
Merlot,'90, Napa Vly. $20.00 (B-Orange)

CYPRESS
1000 Lenzen Ave. San Jose 95126
Cabernet Sauvignon,'89, California $9.00 (B-State Fair)
Merlot,'91, California $9.00 (3)
Sauvignon Blanc,'91, California $6.00 (B-San Fran)
White Zinfandel,'92, California $6.00 (G-Orange)

DALLA VALLE VINEYARDS
7776 Silverado Trail Yountville 94599
Cabernet Sauvignon,'89, Napa Vly. $25.00 (B-San Fran)
Cabernet Sauvignon,'90, Napa Vly. $25.00 (B-San Fran)

DE LOACH VINEYARDS
1791 Olivet Rd. Santa Rosa 95401
Cabernet Sauvignon,'90, Russian River Vly., Estate $16.00 (5)
Chardonnay,'91, Russian River Vly. $15.00 (3)
Gewurztraminer,'91, Russian River Vly., LH $14.00 (4)
Gewurztraminer,'91, Russian River, Early Harvest $8.50 (2)
Gewurztraminer,'92, Russian River Vly., LH $14.00 (2)
Gewurztraminer,'92, Russian River., Early Harvest $8.50 (5)
Pinot Noir,'91, Russian River Vly., (B-State Fair)
Sauvignon Blanc,'91, Russian River Vly. $10.00 (4)
Sauvignon Blanc,'91, Russian River Vly., Fume $10.00 (3)
White Zinfandel,'92, Russian River Vly. $7.50 (2)
Zinfandel,'91, Russian River Vly. $11.50 (G-Dallas)

DE LORIMIER WINERY
P. O. Box 726 Geyserville 95441
Red Meritage,'88, Alexander Vly. Mosaic $18.00 (6)
Semillon,'90, Alexander Vly., Lace, Estate, LH $16.00 (5)
White Meritage,'90, Alexander Vly., Spectrum $10.00 (3)

DE MOOR WINERY
P. O. Box 348 Oakville 94562
Chenin Blanc,'91, Napa Vly. $6.75 (S-Dallas)
Sauvignon Blanc,'91, Napa Vly. (B-State Fair)
Zinfandel,'90, Napa Vly. (B-San Diego)

DE NATALE VINEYARDS
11020 Eastside Rd. Healdsburg 95448
Chardonnay,'91, Russian River Vly., Estate (B-New World)

DECOY
3027 Silverado Trail St Helena 94574
Pinot Noir,'90, Russian River Vly. $11.00 (B-Orange)

DEER PARK WINERY
1000 Deer Park Rd. Deer Park 94576
Sauvignon Blanc,'91, Napa Vly., Estate, LH $10.00 (B-Farmers)
Zinfandel,'89, Howell Mtn. (B-San Diego)
Zinfandel,'89, Howell Mtn., Beatty Ranch Res. (2)

DEER VALLEY VINEYARDS
P.O. Box 780 Gonzales 93926
Cabernet Sauvignon,'89, Monterey Co. $6.00 (2)
Cabernet Sauvignon,'90, Monterey Co. $6.00 (2)
Merlot,'91, Monterey Co. (S-W. Coast)

DELICATO VINEYARDS
12001 S. Hwy. 99 Manteca 95336
Sauvignon Blanc,'91, California, Reserve $6.99 (B-Orange)
Sauvignon Blanc,'91, Monterey $4.99 (B-Orange)
White Zinfandel,'92, California $4.99 (S-Orange)

DEUX AMIS
78670 Welter Lane Sebastopol 95472
Zinfandel,'91, Sonoma Co. (B-State Fair)

DEVLIN WINE CELLARS
P. O. Box 728 Soquel 95073
Chardonnay,'91, Monterey Co. $9.50 (B-Orange)
Chardonnay,'91, Santa Cruz, Beauregard Ranch $9.50 (S-Orange)
Chenin Blanc,'92, Central Coast $4.50 (G-Orange)
Merlot,'91, Central Coast $9.50 (S-Orange)

DICKERSON VINEYARD
Address Not Available
Cabernet Sauvignon,'89, Napa, Ruby, Reserve $10.00 (B-San Fran)

DOLCE
Address Not Available
Semillon,'90, California, LH $99.00 (G-Orange)

DOMAINE BRETON
P. O. Box 1146 Middletown 95461
Chardonnay,'92, California $8.00 (B-New World)
Sauvignon Blanc,'90, North Coast $7.00 (S-New World)

DOMAINE CARNEROS
1240 Duhig Road Napa 94558
Sparkling Wine,'NV, Napa, Carneros, Brut $20.00 (B-San Fran)

DOMAINE CHANDON
California Dr. Yountville 94599
Sparkling Wine,'NV, Carneros, Blanc de Noirs $12.00 (B-Orange)
Sparkling Wine,'NV, Chandon Reserve $17.50 (B-Orange)

DOMAINE DE CLARCK
7023 Carmel Valley Rd. Carmel 93923
Chardonnay,'91, Monterey Co. $14.00 (2)

DOMAINE DU GRAND ARCHER
Address Not Available
Cabernet Sauvignon,'90, Sonoma Co. $11.00 (B-Orange)

DOMAINE MICHEL
4155 Wine Creek Rd. Healdsburg 95448
Cabernet Sauvignon,'89, Sonoma Co. $19.00 (S-State Fair)
Chardonnay,'90, Sonoma Co. $15.00 (B-Dallas)
Chardonnay,'91, Dry Creek Vly. $15.00 (B-State Fair)

DOMAINE MONTREAUX
4101 Big Ranch Road Napa 94558
Sparkling Wine,'86, Napa Vly. (B-W. Coast)

DOMAINE NAPA WINERY
1155 Mee Lane St Helena 94574
Cabernet Sauvignon,'89, Napa Vly. (B-San Diego)
Chardonnay,'91, Napa Vly. $12.50 (B-San Diego)

DOMAINE ST. GEORGE WINERY
1141 Grant Ave. Healdsburg 95448
Cabernet Sauvignon,'88, Alexander Vly., Cuvee, Res, $8.50 (2)
Cabernet Sauvignon,'90, California, Reserve $8.50 (B-Farmers)
Chardonnay,'92, California, Reserve $8.50 (2)
Merlot,'89, Chalk Hill, Premiere Cuvee $8.00 (2)

Sauvignon Blanc,'91, Sonoma Co., Reserve (S-W. Coast)

J. PATRICK DORE WINES
330 Ignacio Blvd. #B-35 Novato 94949
Cabernet Sauvignon,'91, California $5.00 (2)
Chardonnay,'89, Calif., Ltd. Release, Lot 101 (G-New World)
Chardonnay,'91, California (B-New World)
White Zinfandel,'92, California $4.50 (B-Farmers)

DREYER SONOMA WINERY
P. O. Box 789 Glen Ellen 95442
Cabernet Sauvignon,'90, Sonoma Co. (B-State Fair)
Chardonnay,'91, Sonoma Co., Carneros $15.00 (2)

DRY CREEK VINEYARD
3770 Lambert Bridge Healdsburg 95448
Cabernet Franc,'90, Dry Creek Vly. (3)
Cabernet Sauvignon,'90, Dry Creek Vly. $14.00 (5)
Chardonnay,'90, Dry Creek Vly., Reserve $20.00 (4)
Chardonnay,'91, Sonoma Co. $13.00 (4)
Chenin Blanc,'91, California $7.00 (2)
Chenin Blanc,'92, California $7.00 (5)
Merlot,'90, Dry Creek Vly. $14.00 (3)
Red Meritage,'87, Dry Creek Vly. $24.00 (B-New World)
Red Meritage,'88, Dry Creek Vly. $24.00 (2)
Sauvignon Blanc,'91, Sonoma Co., Fume $9.25 (4)
Zinfandel,'90, Dry Creek Vly., Old Vines $11.00 (4)

DUNNEWOOD
3111 N. St. Helena Hwy. St Helena 94574
Cabernet Sauvignon,'89, California, Barrel Select (B-State Fair)
Cabernet Sauvignon,'90, California (G-New World)
Chardonnay,'91, North Coast, Barrel Select (B-New World)
Merlot,'90, California, Barrel Select $6.00 (2)
Sauvignon Blanc,'91, California $6.00 (B-San Fran)

DURNEY VINEYARD
P.O. Box 222016 Carmel 93922
Chardonnay,'90, Carmel Vly., Estate $15.00 (B-San Fran)

DUSINBERRE WINERY
Address Not Available
Sparkling Wine,'90, Napa Vly., Marston Vnyd. (B-San Diego)

E

EAGLE RIDGE WINERY
111 Goodwin Avenue Penngrove 94951
Gewurztraminer,'92, Alexander Vly., Semi-dry $7.50 (S-Orange)
Semillon,'91, Sonoma, LH, Semmelon $25.00 (B-Orange)
Zinfandel,'91, Amador Co., Limited Ed. $15.00 (B-State Fair)

EBERLE WINERY
128 Fairview Paso Robles 93446
Cabernet Sauvignon,'89, Paso Robles, Estate (2)
Syrah,'91, Paso Robles $12.00 (2)
Zinfandel,'90, Paso Robles, Sauret Vnyd. (S-Dallas)

EDMEADES
5500 Hwy. 128 Philo 95466
Chardonnay,'91, Mendocino $16.00 (2)

Zinfandel,'90, Anderson Vly., Ciapusci Vnyd. $16.00 (Σ-San Fran)

ELLISTON VINEYARDS
463 Kilkare Road Sunol 94586
Chardonnay,'91, Central Coast, Sunol Vly. Vnyd. (B-San Diego)
Pinot Blanc,'91, Central Coast, Sunol Vly. Vnyd. (2)

EMERALD BAY
P. O. Box 221775 Carmel 93923
Cabernet Sauvignon,'91, California, Reserve $6.00 (B-Orange)
Chardonnay,'91, California (B-W. Coast)

EPOCH
Address Not Available
Merlot,'89, Paso Robles, Epoch $13.50 (S-Orange)

ESTANCIA WINERY
1178 Galleron Rd. Rutherford 94573
Cabernet Sauvignon,'90, Alexander Vly. $10.00 (2)
Chardonnay,'91, Monterey $9.00 (G-Orange)
Red Meritage,'90, Alexander Vly. $15.00 (6)
Sauvignon Blanc,'91, Monterey Co. $8.00 (5)
White Meritage,'91, Monterey $12.00 (4)

ESTRELLA RIVER
Shandon Star Rte. Paso Robles 93446
Cabernet Sauvignon,'90, California, Prop. Reserve $6.00 (2)
Chenin Blanc,'92, California (B-New World)
White Zinfandel,'92, California $4.50 (3)

EUREKA!
Address Not Available
Chardonnay,'92, North Coast (S-New World)
White Zinfandel,'92, California (B-New World)

EVEREST
Address Not Available
Cabernet Sauvignon,'89, Dry Creek Vly. $15.00 (4)

EYE OF THE SWAN CELLARS
389 Fourth St. E. Sonoma 95476
Cabernet Sauvignon,'89, California $7.00 (S-Orange)
Chardonnay,'91, California (B-New World)

F

FALCONER CELLARS
Address Not Available
Sparkling Wine,'84, Russian Riv, Blanc de Blanc $16.00 (S-San Fran)

FALLENLEAF WINERY
1075 Buchli Station Rd. Napa 94558
Sauvignon Blanc,'91, Sonoma Vly. $9.00 (2)

GARY FARRELL WINES
P. O. Box 342 Forestville 95436
Cabernet Sauvignon,'90, Sonoma Co., Ladi's Vnyd. $18.00 (7)
Chardonnay,'91, Russian River Vly. (S-San Diego)
Chardonnay,'91, Russian River Vly., Allen Vnyd. $18.00 (2)
Merlot,'90, Sonoma Co. Ladi's Vineyard $16.00 (4)
Pinot Noir,'91, Russian River Vly. $16.50 (2)
Pinot Noir,'91, Russian River Vly., Allen Vnyd. $32.00 (8)

Sauvignon Blanc,'92, Russian River Rochioli Vnyd. $10.00 (5)
Zinfandel,'91, Russian River Vly. $14.50 (8)

FENESTRA WINERY

2954 Kilkare Road Sunol 94586

Cabernet Sauvignon,'88, Smith & Hook Vnyd. $15.00 (B-San Diego)
Chardonnay,'91, Livermore Vly., Toy Vnyd. $12.50 (2)
Merlot,'90, Livermore Vly. $13.00 (2)
Semillon,'91, Livermore Vly. $9.00 (4)

FENSALIR CELLARS

680 Rossi St Helena 94574

Cabernet Sauvignon,'89, Napa Vly., Estate (B-Dallas)

FERRARI-CARANO VINEYARD

8761 Dry Creek Road Healdsburg 95448

Sauvignon Blanc,'92, Sonoma Co. Fume $11.00 (S-Orange)

GLORIA FERRER

23555 Highway 121 Sonoma 95476

Chardonnay,'91, Carneros $15.00 (4)
Chardonnay,'91, Napa Vly. (S-W. Coast)
Sparkling Wine,'85, Carneros Cuvee Brut (S-Dallas)
Sparkling Wine,'86, Carneros, Carneros Cuvee $23.00 (4)
Sparkling Wine,'87, Carneros, Royal Cuvee $17.00 (4)
Sparkling Wine,'NV, Sonoma Co., Brut $14.00 (9)

FETZER VINEYARDS

13325 So. Highway 101 Hopland 95449

Cabernet Sauvignon,'86, Sonoma Co., Reserve $22.00 (2)
Cabernet Sauvignon,'87, Sonoma Co., Reserve $22.00 (4)
Cabernet Sauvignon,'89, California, Barrel Select $11.00 (4)
Cabernet Sauvignon,'90, Calif., Barrel Select $11.00 (B-State Fair)
Cabernet Sauvignon,'90, California, Valley Oaks $8.00 (5)
Cabernet Sauvignon,'91, California, Valley Oaks $8.00 (3)
Chardonnay,'90, Mendocino Co. Reserve $19.00 (6)
Chardonnay,'91, California, Sundial $8.00 (B-New World)
Chardonnay,'91, Mendocino Co., Organic $9.00 (G-Orange)
Chardonnay,'91, Mendocino, Barrel Sel. $11.00 (7)
Chardonnay,'92, California, Sundial $8.00 (3)
Gewurztraminer,'92, California $7.00 (8)
Johannisberg Riesling,'91, California $7.00 (2)
Johannisberg Riesling,'92, California $7.00 (4)
Merlot,'90, California Eagle Peak $8.00 (4)
Merlot,'91, California, Eagle Peak $8.00 (3)
Petite Sirah,'90, Mendocino Co., Reserve (2)
Pinot Noir,'90, California, Reserve $19.00 (6)
Pinot Noir,'91, California, Barrel Select $11.00 (4)
Sauvignon Blanc,'91, California, Fume $7.00 (B-New World)
Sauvignon Blanc,'91, Mendocino, Barrel Sel. $9.00 (G-Orange)
Sauvignon Blanc,'92, California Fume $7.00 (2)
White Zinfandel,'92, California $6.75 (3)
Zinfandel,'90, Mendocino Co., Reserve $12.50 (2)
Zinfandel,'90, Mendocino, Barrel Select $9.00 (4)

FIELD STONE WINERY

10075 Highway 128 Healdsburg 95448

Cabernet Sauvignon,'89, Alexander Vly., Reserve $20.00 (G-
Gewurztraminer,'92, Sonoma Co. $9.00 (G-Orange)

Petite Sirah,'90, Alexander Vly., Old Vines, Estate $16.50 (S-Orange)

FIELDBROOK VALLEY WINERY
4241 Fieldbrook Rd. Fieldbrook 95521
Cabernet Sauvignon,'91, Dry Creek Vly., Opatz Vnyd. (B-State Fair)
Chenin Blanc,'92, Napa Vly., Frediani Vnyd. $6.25 (B-Orange)
Merlot,'91, Napa Vly. $14.00 (S-San Fran)
Pinot Noir,'90, Napa Vly., Beard Vnyd. $12.00 (2)
Red Meritage,'90, North Coast $14.00 (B-San Fran)
Sauvignon Blanc,'92, Mendo., Quillen Vnyd. $10.00 (B-Farmers)

JOSEPH FILIPPI
P.O. Box 2 Mira Loma 91752
Cabernet Franc,'89, Napa Vly. $7.50 (B-Orange)
Gewurztraminer,'NV, California $5.00 (S-Orange)

FILSINGER VINEYARDS
39050 DePortola Rd. Temecula 92390
Cabernet Sauvignon,'89, Temecula, Estate $14.00 (B-Orange)
Sauvignon Blanc,'91, Temecula, Estate Fume $5.50 (G-Orange)
Sparkling Wine,'NV, California Diamond Cuvee $15.00 (B-Farmers)

FIRESTONE VINEYARD
5017 Zaca Station Rd. Los Olivos 93441
Cabernet Sauvignon,'90, Santa Ynez Vly. $12.00 (3)
Cabernet Sauvignon,'90, Santa Ynez, Res. $20.00 (Σ-New World)
Chardonnay,'91, Santa Ynez Vly., Barrel Ferm. $12.50 (S-Farmers)
Chardonnay,'92, Santa Ynez Vly. $12.50 (S-State Fair)
Gewurztraminer,'92, California $9.00 (2)
Johannisberg Riesling,'91, Santa Barbara Co. $7.50 (S-W. Coast)
Johannisberg Riesling,'91, Santa Ynez Vly. $7.50 (2)
Johannisberg Riesling,'92, Santa Ynez Vly. $7.50 (B-W. Coast)
Merlot,'91, Santa Ynez Vly. $12.00 (2)
Sauvignon Blanc,'92, Santa Ynez Vly. $7.50 (B-Farmers)

FISHER VINEYARDS
6200 St. Helena Rd. Santa Rosa 95404
Chardonnay,'91, Sonoma, Coach Insignia $16.00 (B-San Fran)

FITZPATRICK WINERY
6881 Fairplay Rd. Somerset 95684
Cabernet Sauvignon,'81, Tehama, Mt. Lassen Vnyd. (S-State Fair)

FLORA SPRINGS
1078 W. Zinfandel Lane St Helena 94574
Cabernet Sauvignon,'89, Napa, Reserve $38.00 (2)
Merlot,'91, Napa, Floreal $12.00 (3)
Red Meritage,'89, Napa Vly., Trilogy $33.00 (3)

THOMAS FOGARTY WINERY
5937 Alpine Road Portola Valley 94025
Cabernet Sauvignon,'86, Napa Vly. $17.00 (B-San Diego)
Cabernet Sauvignon,'87, Napa Vly. $17.00 (G-San Fran)
Chardonnay,'90, Edna Vly. Vnyds. (B-New World)
Chardonnay,'90, Santa Cruz Mtns. $18.00 (G-New World)
Gewurztraminer,'92, Monterey, Ventana Vnyd. $11.50 (4)

FOLIE A DEUX WINERY
3070 St. Helena Highway St Helena 94574
Chardonnay,'90, Napa Vly. $16.50 (B-San Diego)
Chenin Blanc,'91, Napa Vly. $8.00 (B-San Diego)

FOPPIANO VINEYARDS
12707 Old Redwood Hwy. Healdsburg 95448
Petite Sirah,'90, Sonoma Co. $10.00 (B-Dallas)

FOREST GLEN WINERY
P. O. Box 789 Ceres 95307
Cabernet Sauvignon,'90, Sonoma Co., Barrel Select $12.00 (5)
Chardonnay,'91, California, Barrel Ferm. $12.00 (8)

FOREST LAKE VINEYARD
Address Not Available
Cabernet Sauvignon,'90, California $6.00 (S-New World)
White Zinfandel,'92, California $5.00 (S-State Fair)

FORTINO WINERY
4525 Hecker Pass Hwy. Gilroy 95020
Cabernet Sauvignon,'84, California (S-State Fair)
Pinot Noir,'90, Santa Clara Vly. $8.50 (B-Orange)

FOXEN
Rt. 1, Box 144-A Santa Maria 93454
Cabernet Sauvignon,'90, Santa Barbara Co. $20.00 (S-Orange)

FRANCISCAN OAKVILLE ESTATE
1178 Galleron Rd. Rutherford 94573
Cabernet Sauvignon,'89, Napa Vly. (B-State Fair)
Chardonnay,'91, Napa Vly. (4)
Chardonnay,'91, Napa Vly., Cuvee Sauvage $24.00 (4)
Merlot,'90, Napa Vly. $14.50 (3)
Red Meritage,'89, Napa Vly. Magnificant $20.00 (7)
Zinfandel,'91, Napa Vly. $10.00 (4)

FRANZIA BROTHERS WINERY
1700 E. Hwy. 120 Ripon 95366
Cabernet Sauvignon,'NV, California (B-State Fair)

FRATELLI PERATA
1595 Arbor Road Paso Robles 93446
Cabernet Sauvignon,'90, Paso Robles, Estate $12.75 (B-Farmers)

FREEMARK ABBEY
3020 St. Helena Hwy., No. St Helena 94574
Cabernet Sauvignon,'87, Napa Vly., Boche $26.00 (B-L.A.)
Cabernet Sauvignon,'88, Napa Vly. $16.00 (B-Farmers)
Cabernet Sauvignon,'89, Napa Vly. $16.00 (B-State Fair)
Chardonnay,'90, Napa Vly. $15.00 (2)
Chardonnay,'90, Napa Vly., Carpy Ranch $22.00 (B-San Diego)
Johannisberg Riesling,'91, Napa, Edelwein Gold $25.00 (2)

FREMONT CREEK WINERY
Address Not Available
Chardonnay,'91, North Coast, Beckstoffer Vnyds. (S-State Fair)

FRICK
303 Potrero St. #39 Santa Cruz 95060
Zinfandel,'90, Russian River Vly. (S-San Diego)

J. FRITZ WINERY
24691 Dutcher Creek Cloverdale 95425
Chardonnay,'91, Russian River Vly., Barrel Select $12.50 (S-Dallas)
Chardonnay,'91, Sonoma Co. $9.50 (4)

Sauvignon Blanc,'92, Dry Creek Vly. $8.00 (2)
Zinfandel,'90, Dry Creek, 80 Year Old Vines $10.00 (2)
Zinfandel,'91, 80 Year Old Vines $10.00 (S-San Diego)

J. FURST
Address Not Available
Chardonnay,'91, California $9.00 (4)
Pinot Noir,'91, Sonoma Co. $9.00 (2)
Sauvignon Blanc,'91, California, Fume $9.00 (4)
White Zinfandel,'92, California $7.00 (3)

G

GABRIELLI WINERY
10950 West Road   Redwood Valley   95470
Chardonnay,'91, Mendocino Co. $16.00 (2)
Chardonnay,'91, Mendocino, Reserve $20.00 (S-Orange)
Zinfandel,'90, Mendocino Co. $10.00 (2)
Zinfandel,'91, Mendocino Co. $10.00 (S-State Fair)
Zinfandel,'91, Mendocino Co., Reserve (B-State Fair)

GAINEY VINEYARD
P. O. Box 910   Santa Ynez   93460
Cabernet Sauvignon,'89, Santa Ynez Vly. $13.00 (B-W. Coast)
Chardonnay,'91, Santa Barbara Co. $13.00 (3)
Johannisberg Riesling,'92, Santa Ynez Vly. $8.00 (S-State Fair)
Merlot,'90, Santa Ynez Vly. (2)
Pinot Noir,'90, Santa Barbara Co. $15.00 (2)
Sauvignon Blanc,'91, Santa Ynez Vly. $9.00 (5)
Sauvignon Blanc,'91, Santa Ynez, Ltd. Selection $16.00 (B-San Fran)

E. & J. GALLO
P. O. Box 1130   Modesto   95353
White Zinfandel,'92, California $4.50 (B-Orange)

GAN EDEN
4950 Ross Road   Sebastopol   95472
Cabernet Sauvignon,'88, Alexander Vly. $18.00 (B-Orange)
Chardonnay,'90, Alex. Vly./Mendocino, Res. $16.00 (4)
Gewurztraminer,'92, Russian River Vly., LH $8.00 (6)

GARLAND RANCH
P. O. Box 221755   Carmel   93923
Cabernet Sauvignon,'91, California $7.00 (2)
Chardonnay,'92, California $7.00 (B-New World)
Merlot,'91, California $7.00 (2)

GAVILAN
P. O. Box 855   Soledad   93960
Pinot Blanc,'92, Monterey, Pinnacles, Soledad $12.50 (B-Orange)

GEMELLO WINERY
2003 El Camino Real   Mountain View   94040
Zinfandel,'90, Mendocino Co. (S-State Fair)

GEYSER PEAK WINERY
22281 Chianti Rd.   Geyserville   95441
Cabernet Franc,'89, Alexander Vly. $9.00 (4)
Cabernet Sauvignon,'90, Alexander Vly., Reserve $15.00 (5)
Cabernet Sauvignon,'90, Sonoma Co. $9.00 (3)
Chardonnay,'91, Alexander Vly., Reserve $15.00 (3)

Chardonnay,'91, Sonoma Co. $9.00 (5)
Gewurztraminer,'92, Sonoma Co. $5.50 (8)
Johannisberg Riesling,'92, Soft, North Coast $5.50 (8)
Merlot,'91, Alexander Vly. $12.00 (5)
Petite Sirah,'90, Alexander Vly. $15.00 (2)
Red Meritage,'90, Reserve Alexandre $21.00 (8)
Sauvignon Blanc,'92, Sonoma Co. $6.50 (7)
Semillon,'92, Semchard, California $6.50 (9)
Syrah,'91, Alexander Vly., Reserve $12.00 (5)
Zinfandel,'90, Dry Creek Vly. $9.00 (3)

GIRARD WINERY
7717 Silverado Trail Oakville 94562
Cabernet Sauvignon,'89, Napa Vly., Estate $16.00 (S-San Fran)

GLASS MOUNTAIN
Address Not Available
Cabernet Sauvignon,'90, California (B-State Fair)

GLASS MOUNTAIN QUARRY
P. O. Box 636 St Helena 94574
Petite Sirah,'90, Napa Vly. $9.00 (G-Orange)

GLEN ELLEN WINERY
1883 London Ranch Rd. Glen Ellen 95442
Cabernet Sauvignon,'91, Calif., Prop. Reserve $6.00 (G-Orange)
Chardonnay,'92, California, Prop. Reserve $6.00 (7)
Merlot,'91, California, Prop. Reserve $6.00 (5)
Sauvignon Blanc,'92, California $4.99 (2)
White Zinfandel,'92, California, Prop. Reserve $5.00 (7)

GOLD HILL VINEYARD
5660 Vineyard Lane Coloma 95613
Chardonnay,'90, El Dorado $10.00 (B-State Fair)
Merlot,'90, El Dorado Co. $11.00 (3)
Red Meritage,'89, El Dorado $16.00 (B-San Fran)

GOLDEN CREEK VINEYARD
4480 Wallace Road Santa Rosa 95404
Cabernet Sauvignon,'90, Sonoma Co. $12.00 (6)
Merlot,'90, Sonoma Co. $12.00 (5)
Red Meritage,'90, Sonoma Co. Caberlot $12.00 (7)

GOLDEN STATE VINTNERS
38558 Road 128 Cutler 93615
Chardonnay,'92, California (B-San Diego)

GOOSECROSS CELLARS
1119 State Lane Yountville 94599
Chardonnay,'90, Napa Vly. $9.00 (S-New World)

GRAESER WINERY
255 Petrified Forest Rd. Calistoga 94515
Cabernet Franc,'89, Napa Vly., Estate $14.00 (5)

GRAND CRU VINEYARDS
1 Vintage Lane Glen Ellen 95442
Cabernet Sauvignon,'90, California, Premium Selection $8.00 (2)
Chardonnay,'91, California $8.00 (6)
Chenin Blanc,'92, California, Premium Selection $6.50 (2)
Johannisberg Riesling,'91, California $6.50 (2)

Sauvignon Blanc,'90, Sonoma Co., Premium Sel. $6.50 (S-Dallas)
Sauvignon Blanc,'91, California $6.50 (3)
White Zinfandel,'92, California $6.50 (6)

GRANITE SPRINGS WINERY
6060 Granite Springs Road Somerset 95684
Cabernet Franc,'90, El Dorado, Estate $12.50 (3)
Petite Sirah,'90, El Dorado Co., Granite Hill $10.00 (2)
Petite Sirah,'91, El Dorado $10.00 (3)
Zinfandel,'90, El Dorado Co., Estate $8.50 (5)

GREEN & RED VINEYARD
32080 Chiles Pope Valley Rd. St Helena 94574
Zinfandel,'91, Napa Vly., Chiles Mill Vnyd. $13.00 (2)

GREENSTONE
P.O. Box 1164 Ione 95640
Chenin Blanc,'92, Amador Co. $5.00 (3)
White Zinfandel,'92, Amador Co. (B-State Fair)

GREENWOOD RIDGE VINEYARDS
24555 Greenwood Rd. Philo 95466
Cabernet Sauvignon,'89, Anderson Vly. $12.00 (B-State Fair)
Chardonnay,'91, Mendocino Co. $16.00 (5)
Johannisberg Riesling,'92, Anderson Vly., White $8.50 (4)
Pinot Noir,'91, Mendocino Co. $15.00 (3)
Sauvignon Blanc,'91, Anderson Vly. $8.50 (4)
Zinfandel,'91, Sonoma Co., Sherrer Vnyds. $12.50 (3)

GRGICH HILLS CELLAR
1829 St. Helena Hwy. Rutherford 94573
Cabernet Sauvignon,'87, Napa Vly. $30.00 (5)
Chardonnay,'90, Napa Vly. $22.00 (4)
Sauvignon Blanc,'91, Napa Vly., Fume $11.00 (5)
Zinfandel,'88, Sonoma Co. $13.00 (B-New World)
Zinfandel,'89, Sonoma Co. $13.00 (4)

GROTH VINEYARDS
750 Oakville Cross Oakville 94562
Chardonnay,'91, Napa Vly. $13.50 (B-Orange)

GUENOC WINERY
21000 Butts Canyon Rd. Middletown 95461
Cabernet Franc,'90, Napa Vly. (2)
Cabernet Sauvignon,'88, Lake Co./Napa Co. (S-L.A.)
Cabernet Sauvignon,'89, Napa, Beckstoffer Reserve $30.00 (2)
Cabernet Sauvignon,'90, Napa, Beckstoffer, Reserve $35.00 (4)
Chardonnay,'89, Genevieve Magoon Res. $22.00 (4)
Chardonnay,'90, Genevieve Magoon Res. $22.00 (2)
Chardonnay,'90, Guenoc Vly., Estate $14.00 (B-San Diego)
Chardonnay,'90, North Coast $11.00 (S-L.A.)
Chardonnay,'91, Genevieve Magoon Res. $22.00 (5)
Chardonnay,'91, Guenoc Vly., Estate $14.00 (2)
Chardonnay,'92, Genevieve Magoon Reserve (S-L.A.)
Chardonnay,'92, North Coast $11.00 (2)
Chenin Blanc,'90, California (B-Dallas)
Petite Sirah,'88, Guenoc Vly. (2)
Petite Sirah,'89, North Coast $13.00 (3)
Petite Sirah,'90, North Coast $13.00 (5)
Red Meritage,'88, Napa County/Lake County $35.00 (2)

Red Meritage,'89, Lake County $15.00 (4)
Sauvignon Blanc,'90, Guenoc Vly., Estate $10.00 (2)
Sauvignon Blanc,'91, Guenoc Vly., Estate $10.00 (3)
Sauvignon Blanc,'91, North Coast $7.50 (B-New World)
Sauvignon Blanc,'92, North Coast $7.50 (B-Farmers)
Zinfandel,'89, California (B-New World)
Zinfandel,'90, California (3)

GUGLIELMO WINERY
1480 East Main Ave.   Morgan Hill   95037
Cabernet Sauvignon,'86, Santa Clara Vly., Reserve $12.00 (2)
Chardonnay,'92, Monterey Co., Mt. Madonna $8.25 (3)
Johannisberg Riesling,'92, Mt. Madonna (B-L.A.)
Merlot,'91, Napa Vly., Mt. Madonna (2)
Zinfandel,'88, Santa Clara Vly., Reserve $8.75 (S-Farmers)

GUNDLACH-BUNDSCHU
3775 Thornberry Road   Sonoma   95476
Cabernet Franc,'90, Sonoma Vly., Rhinefarm Vnyds. $14.00 (5)
Cabernet Sauvignon,'90, Sonoma Vly., Rhinefarm Vnyds. $15.00 (3)
Chardonnay,'91, Sangiacomo Ranch $14.00 (5)
Chardonnay,'91, Sonoma Vly. $12.00 (B-State Fair)
Gewurztraminer,'92, Sonoma Vly., Rhinefarm $8.00 (3)
Johannisberg Riesling,'92, Sonoma Vly., Dresel's, Estate $9.00 (4)
Merlot,'90, Sonoma, Rhinefarm Vnyds. $16.00 (2)
Pinot Noir,'91, Sonoma Vly., Rhinefarm Vnyd. $14.00 (B-State Fair)
Zinfandel,'91, Sonoma Vly. $10.00 (2)

H

HACIENDA WINERY
1000 Vineyard Lane   Sonoma   95476
Cabernet Sauvignon,'87, Sonoma Co. $15.00 (S-San Diego)
Cabernet Sauvignon,'90, Sonoma Co. $15.00 (G-New World)
Cabernet Sauvignon,'91, Sonoma Co. $15.00 (B-State Fair)
Chenin Blanc,'91, Clarksburg $6.50 (S-New World)
Chenin Blanc,'92, Clarksburg $6.50 (B-San Diego)

HAGAFEN CELLARS
P. O. Box 3035   Napa   94558
Cabernet Sauvignon,'88, Napa Vly., Reserve $20.00 (B-San Diego)
Chardonnay,'90, Napa Vly., Reserve $17.00 (B-Farmers)
Chardonnay,'91, Napa Vly. $14.00 (S-San Fran)

HAHN ESTATES
P. O. Drawer C   Soledad   93960
Chardonnay,'91, Monterey $9.00 (3)

HANDLEY CELLARS
P. O. Box 66   Philo   95466
Chardonnay,'90, Anderson Vly. $11.00 (4)
Chardonnay,'90, Dry Creek Vly. $14.50 (3)
Chardonnay,'91, Dry Creek Vly. $14.50 (B-San Diego)
Gewurztraminer,'92, Anderson Vly. $8.00 (6)
Pinot Noir,'91, Anderson Vly. $12.50 (5)
Sauvignon Blanc,'91, Dry Creek Vly. $8.00 (6)
Sparkling Wine,'88, Anderson Vly., Blanc de Blanc $18.00 (3)
Sparkling Wine,'88, Anderson Vly., Brut $15.00 (2)
Sparkling Wine,'88, Anderson Vly., Brut Rose (B-Dallas)

Sparkling Wine,'89, Anderson Vly., Brut $15.00 (S-State Fair)
Sparkling Wine,'89, Anderson Vly., Brut Rose (2)

HANNA WINERY
4345 Occidental Rd. Santa Rosa 95401
Chardonnay,'90, Sonoma Co. $13.50 (B-San Diego)
Chardonnay,'91, Sonoma Co. $13.50 (5)
Merlot,'90, Alexander Vly. (S-Dallas)
Sauvignon Blanc,'90, Sonoma Co. $9.65 (2)
Sauvignon Blanc,'92, Sonoma Co. $9.65 (4)

HARMONY CELLARS
P. O. Box 2502 Harmony 93435
Cabernet Sauvignon,'89, Paso Robles $12.00 (S-Dallas)
Cabernet Sauvignon,'90, Paso Robles $12.00 (B-New World)
Johannisberg Riesling,'92, Paso Robles $8.00 (4)
White Zinfandel,'92, Paso Robles $6.00 (5)

HARRISON
Address Not Available
Cabernet Sauvignon,'90, Napa $30.00 (S-San Fran)

HART WINERY
32580 Rancho Calif. Rd. Temecula 92390
Merlot,'90, Temecula (S-New World)

HART'S DESIRE
Address Not Available
Chardonnay,'91, California $9.50 (B-Orange)

HAVENS WINE CELLARS
1441 Calistoga Avenue Napa 94558
Cabernet Franc,'90, Carneros $16.00 (B-Orange)
Merlot,'90, Napa Vly. $15.50 (S-Orange)

HAWK CREST
5766 Silverado Trail Napa 94558
Cabernet Sauvignon,'90, California $9.00 (B-Farmers)
Chardonnay,'92, California $9.00 (3)

HAYWOOD WINERY
18701 Gehricke Rd. Sonoma 95476
Cabernet Sauvignon,'90, California, Vintner's Select (S-New World)
Chardonnay,'91, California, Vintner's Select $8.00 (S-New World)
Zinfandel,'90, Sonoma Vly., Estate $14.00 (S-L.A.)

HEALDSBURG WINE CELLARS
Address Not Available
Zinfandel,'90, Mendocino Co., Bottling 116 (B-New World)

HESS COLLECTION
4140 Redwood Road Napa 94558
Cabernet Sauvignon,'89, Napa Vly. $16.25 (2)
Cabernet Sauvignon,'90, California $9.50 (B-Orange)
Chardonnay,'91, California $9.50 (B-Orange)

HIDDEN CELLARS
1500 Ruddick-Cunningham Rd. Ukiah 95482
Chardonnay,'91, Mendocino Co., Reserve $16.00 (3)
Chardonnay,'92, Organic (B-L.A.)
Johannisberg Riesling,'92, Mendocino Co. $8.00 (6)
Sauvignon Blanc,'91, California $9.00 (2)

White Meritage,'91, Mendocino Co., Alchemy $18.00 (5)
Zinfandel,'90, Mendocino Co. $11.00 (4)

WILLIAM HILL WINERY
1775 Lincoln Ave. Napa 94558
Cabernet Sauvignon,'89, Napa, Reserve $24.00 (B-L.A.)
Sauvignon Blanc,'92, Napa $9.00 (S-L.A.)

HOP KILN WINERY
6050 Westside Rd. Healdsburg 95448
Cabernet Sauvignon,'90, Russian River Vly. $14.00 (5)
Chardonnay,'91, Russian River, Griffin Vnyds. $15.00 (2)
Gewurztraminer,'92, Russian River, Griffin Vnyds. $7.50 (5)
Johannisberg Riesling,'92, M. Griffin Vnyds. $8.00 (B-Farmers)
Petite Sirah,'91, Sonoma Co. $15.00 (5)
Zinfandel,'90, Sonoma Co. $12.00 (5)
Zinfandel,'90, Sonoma Co., Primitivo $15.00 (2)
Zinfandel,'91, Russian River Vly., LH $15.00 (5)
Zinfandel,'91, Sonoma Co., Primitivo $15.00 (5)

HOPE FARMS WINERY
P. O. Box 3620 Paso Robles 93447
Chardonnay,'91, Central Coast $9.95 (B-Orange)
Red Meritage,'91, Paso Robles, Claret $11.95 (B-Orange)

HUNTINGTON
18700 Geyserville Ave. Geyserville 95441
Chardonnay,'91, Alexander Vly. $7.00 (B-Orange)

HUSCH VINEYARDS
4400 Highway 128 Philo 95466
Cabernet Sauvignon,'88, North Field Select $18.00 (S-Orange)
Cabernet Sauvignon,'89, Mendocino, La Ribera Vnyds. $14.00 (3)
Cabernet Sauvignon,'89, Mendocino, North Field Sel. $18.00 (4)
Cabernet Sauvignon,'90, Mendocino, La Ribera Vnyd. $14.00 (2)
Chardonnay,'91, Mendocino, Estate $11.00 (2)
Chenin Blanc,'91, Mendocino, La Ribera Vnyd. $7.50 (2)
Chenin Blanc,'92, Mendocino, La Ribera Vnyd. $7.50 (4)
Gewurztraminer,'91, Anderson Vly. $8.50 (5)
Pinot Noir,'90, Anderson Vly., Estate $14.00 (2)
Sauvignon Blanc,'91, La Ribera Vnyd. $8.50 (G-New World)
Sauvignon Blanc,'92, Mendocino, La Ribera Vnyd $8.50 (5)

IMAGERY SERIES
1883 London Ranch Rd. Glen Ellen 95442
Cabernet Franc,'89, Alex. Vly., Blue Rock Vnyd. $16.00 (2)
Petite Sirah,'89, California $16.00 (3)
Petite Sirah,'90, Shell Creek Vnyds. $16.00 (S-San Diego)
Syrah,'90, (G-L.A.)

INDIAN SPRINGS VINEYARDS
16110 Indian Springs Rd. Penn Valley 95946
Cabernet Sauvignon,'89, Sierra Foothills $10.00 (3)
Chardonnay,'91, Sierra Foothills, Reserve $16.00 (2)
Merlot,'90, Nevada Co. $12.00 (B-Farmers)
Merlot,'91, Nevada Co. $12.00 (2)

NGLENOOK-NAPA VALLEY
1991 St. Helena Hwy. Rutherford 94573
Cabernet Sauvignon,'87, Napa Vly., Reserve $17.00 (B-State Fair)
Chenin Blanc,'NV, California, Premium, Select $2.00 (B-Orange)
Merlot,'88, Napa Vly., Reserve $12.00 (S-San Fran)

RON HORSE VINEYARDS
9786 Ross Station Road Sebastopol 95472
Sparkling Wine,'87, Green Vly., Brut, Estate $28.00 (S-Orange)
Sparkling Wine,'89, Green Vly., Brut, Estate $23.00 (G-Orange)
Sparkling Wine,'NV, Green Vly., Vrais Amis $23.00 (G-Orange)
Sparkling Wine,'NV, Green Vly., Wedding Cuvee $23.00 (B-Orange)

J

1474 Alexander Vly. Rd. Healdsburg 95448
Sparkling Wine,'88, Sonoma Co. $23.00 (2)
Sparkling Wine,'89, Sonoma Co. Brut $23.00 (3)

HOMAS JAEGER WINERY
13455 San Pasqual Rd. Escondido 92025
Merlot,'88, Napa Vly., Inglewood Vnyd. $15.00 (B-San Diego)

OBIN JAMES
P. O. Box 2459 Paso Robles 93447
Merlot,'91, Paso Robles, Full Moon $14.00 (2)
Pinot Noir,'90, Santa Barbara Co., Sunshine $15.00 (B-Dallas)
Zinfandel,'91, Paso Robles, Big Time $12.00 (B-San Fran)
Zinfandel,'91, Paso Robles, Blue Moon Res. $14.00 (B-San Fran)

ANKRIS VINEYARD
Rt. 2, Box 40 Templeton 93465
Merlot,'91, Paso Robles $9.00 (3)
Zinfandel,'91, Paso Robles $8.50 (2)

EKEL VINEYARDS
40155 Walnut Avenue Greenfield 93927
Cabernet Franc,'90, Monterey $15.00 (S-State Fair)
Cabernet Sauvignon,'89, Arroyo Seco, Library $10.00 (B-San Fran)
Cabernet Sauvignon,'90, Arroyo Seco, Estate $9.95 (B-Orange)
Chardonnay,'89, Arroyo Seco, Sanctuary, Sceptre (2)
Chardonnay,'90, Arroyo Seco, Estate $12.00 (S-San Diego)
Chardonnay,'91, Arroyo Seco $12.00 (S-State Fair)
Merlot,'90, Monterey $10.95 (3)
Red Meritage,'89, Arroyo Seco, Symmetry $20.00 (2)

EPSON VINEYARDS
10400 So. Highway 101 Ukiah 95482
Chardonnay,'89, Mendocino $13.50 (B-Farmers)
Chardonnay,'90, Mendocino $13.50 (B-State Fair)
Sauvignon Blanc,'90, Mendocino $8.50 (3)
Sparkling Wine,'88, Mendocino, Blanc de Blanc $16.00 (3)

J WINERY
6342 Bystrum Road Ceres 95307
Sparkling Wine,'NV, California Champagne (S-State Fair)

ORDON VINEYARD
1474 Alexander Vly. Rd. Healdsburg 95448
Cabernet Sauvignon,'89, Alexander Vly., Estate (B-Dallas)

JOULLIAN VINEYARD
20300 Cachagua Rd. Carmel Valley 93924
Cabernet Sauvignon,'89, Carmel Vly. $14.00 (4)
Chardonnay,'91, Carmel Vly., Family Reserve (S-State Fair)
Chardonnay,'91, Monterey $10.50 (6)
Sauvignon Blanc,'91, Carmel Vly. $6.50 (2)

JUSTIN VINEYARDS
11680 Chimney Rock Rd. Paso Robles 93446
Cabernet Sauvignon,'89, Paso Robles $18.00 (B-W. Coast)
Red Meritage,'89, Paso Robles Isosceles Res. $22.50 (2)

K

KARLY WINERY
11076 Bell Rd. Plymouth 95669
Petite Sirah,'91, Amador Co. (B-W. Coast)
Sauvignon Blanc,'91, Amador Co. $9.00 (2)

KAUTZ IRONSTONE
1894 Six Mile Rd. Murphys 95247
Cabernet Sauvignon,'88, California $10.00 (B-San Fran)
Chardonnay,'90, Sierra Foothills (B-State Fair)
Merlot,'90, California, "Highlands" $10.00 (2)

ROBERT KEENAN WINERY
3660 Spring Mtn. Rd. St Helena 94574
Cabernet Franc,'89, Napa Vly. $18.00 (4)
Cabernet Sauvignon,'89, Napa Vly. $18.00 (S-Orange)
Chardonnay,'91, Napa Vly. (2)
Merlot,'89, Napa Vly. (S-New World)
Merlot,'90, Napa Vly. $18.00 (4)

KENDALL-JACKSON WINERY
640 Mathews Rd. Lakeport 95453
Cabernet Sauvignon,'88, Calif., Grand Reserve $30.00 (2)
Cabernet Sauvignon,'89, California (B-W. Coast)
Cabernet Sauvignon,'90, Calif., Prop. Grand Reserve (B-State Fair)
Cabernet Sauvignon,'90, California, Vintner's Reserve (2)
Chardonnay,'91, Calif., Prop. Grand Reserve $23.00 (5)
Chardonnay,'91, California, Vintner's Reserve $13.00 (B-Farmers)
Chardonnay,'91, Santa Maria, Camelot Vnyd. $14.00 (2)
Chardonnay,'92, California, Vintner's Reserve $13.00 (3)
Johannisberg Riesling,'92, California, Vintner's Reserve (2)
Merlot,'90, California Vintner's Reserve $14.00 (3)
Merlot,'91, California, Vintner's Reserve $14.00 (3)
Pinot Noir,'90, Calif., Vintner's Reserve (B-New World)
Pinot Noir,'91, Calif., Grand Reserve $30.00 (4)
Pinot Noir,'91, Calif., Vintner's Reserve $13.00 (3)
Red Meritage,'88, California, Cardinale $50.00 (2)
Sauvignon Blanc,'91, Calif., Vintner's Reserve $9.00 (4)
Sauvignon Blanc,'92, California, Vintner's Reserve (2)
Syrah,'89, Sonoma Vly., Durell Vnyd. (2)
Syrah,'90, Calif., Prop. Grand Reserve (S-Dallas)
Syrah,'90, California, Vintner's Reserve $13.00 (2)
White Meritage,'91, California, Royale $15.00 (4)
Zinfandel,'88, Mendocino, Ciapusci Vnyd. $20.00 (2)
Zinfandel,'89, Anderson Vly., DuPratt Vnyd. $16.00 (4)

Zinfandel,'89, Mendocino Co., Ciapusci $20.00 (5)
Zinfandel,'90, Calif., Prop. Grand Reserve $20.00 (2)
Zinfandel,'90, California, Vintner's Reserve (2)
Zinfandel,'91, California, Vintner's Reserve $10.00 (4)

ATHRYN KENNEDY WINERY
13180 Pierce Rd. Saratoga 95070
Cabernet Sauvignon,'89, Santa Cruz Mtns. $54.00 (3)
Red Meritage,'91, California, Lateral $17.50 (5)

ENWOOD VINEYARDS
9592 Sonoma Highway Kenwood 94552
Cabernet Sauvignon,'89, Sonoma Vly. $15.00 (2)
Cabernet Sauvignon,'89, Sonoma Vly., Jack London $20.00 (5)
Chardonnay,'91, Sonoma Vly., Reserve (2)
Merlot,'90, Sonoma Co. $15.00 (2)
Merlot,'90, Sonoma Mtn., Jack London $20.00 (B-Orange)
Pinot Noir,'91, Sonoma Mtn., Jack London $17.50 (3)
Sauvignon Blanc,'91, Sonoma Co. $9.50 (5)
Zinfandel,'90, Sonoma Vly., Jack London $14.00 (2)
Zinfandel,'91, Sonoma Mtn., Jack Londn $14.00 (B-L.A.)

ONOCTI WINERY
4350 Thomas Dr. Kelseyville 95451
Cabernet Franc,'89, Lake Co. $10.00 (5)
Chardonnay,'92, Lake Co. $9.00 (4)
Johannisberg Riesling,'92, Lake Co. $7.50 (4)
Merlot,'91, Lake Co. $10.00 (B-Farmers)
Sauvignon Blanc,'91, Lake Co., Fume $7.50 (4)
White Meritage,'89, Clear Lake, Estate (B-New World)
White Meritage,'91, Clear Lake, Mt. Konocti, Select $14.00 (4)

ONRAD ESTATE
3620 Road B Redwood Valley 95470
Chardonnay,'90, Mendocino Co. $10.00 (B-Farmers)
Chardonnay,'91, Mendocino Co. $12.00 (3)
Red Meritage,'89, Melange a Trois $12.00 (2)
Zinfandel,'90, Mendocino Co. $8.50 (4)

ORBEL
13250 River Rd. Forestville 95446
Cabernet Sauvignon,'90, Alexander Vly. (S-L.A.)
Chardonnay,'91, Sonoma Co. $10.00 (5)
Sauvignon Blanc,'91, Alexander Vly. (2)
Sparkling Wine,'NV, California Rouge $11.00 (2)
Sparkling Wine,'NV, California, Blanc de Noirs $13.00 (5)
Sparkling Wine,'NV, California, Brut $13.00 (2)
Sparkling Wine,'NV, California, Extra Dry $11.00 (2)
Sparkling Wine,'NV, California, Natural $13.00 (6)

HARLES KRUG WINERY
2800 Main Street St Helena 94574
Cabernet Sauvignon,'86, Napa Vly., Vintage Select (S-L.A.)
Cabernet Sauvignon,'89, Napa Vly., Estate $12.00 (3)
Chardonnay,'91, Napa Vly., Estate (B-San Diego)
Chenin Blanc,'92, Napa Vly. $6.50 (3)
Merlot,'90, Napa Vly., Estate $13.25 (3)
Pinot Noir,'90, Napa Vly., Carneros (B-State Fair)

KUNDE ESTATE WINERY
10155 Sonoma Hwy. Kenwood 95474
Cabernet Sauvignon,'90, Sonoma Vly., Estate (B-San Diego)
Chardonnay,'91, Sonoma Vly., Estate $15.00 (B-Orange)
Sauvignon Blanc,'91, Sonoma Vly., Magnolia Lane (B-San Diego)

LA CASA SENA/ASHLY VINEYARD
Address Not Available
Chardonnay,'91, Monterey (B-State Fair)

LA CREMA WINERY
971 Transport Way Petaluma 94953
Chardonnay,'91, California, Reserve $19.00 (G-State Fair)
Pinot Noir,'91, California, Reserve $19.00 (2)

LA CROSSE
Address Not Available
Chardonnay,'92, Napa Vly. (G-State Fair)

LA JOTA VINEYARD
1102 Las Posadas Rd. Angwin 94508
Cabernet Sauvignon,'88, Napa Vly., Howell Mtn. $25.00 (B-Orange)

LAKE SONOMA WINERY
P.O. Box 263 Healdsburg 95448
Sauvignon Blanc,'92, Dry Creek, Polson Vnyds., LH $21.50 (S-
Zinfandel,'92, Dry Creek, Polson Vnyds., LH $21.50 (S-Orange)

LAKESPRING WINERY
2055 Hoffman Lane Napa 94558
Cabernet Sauvignon,'90, Napa Vly. (S-L.A.)
Chardonnay,'90, Napa Vly. (B-W. Coast)
Sauvignon Blanc,'92, Napa Vly., Yount Mill Vnyd. $8.50 (2)

LAKEWOOD VINEYARDS
640 Mathews Rd. Lakeport 95453
Semillon,'91, Clear Lake $12.00 (2)
White Meritage,'91, Clear Lake $12.00 (B-San Fran)

LANDMARK VINEYARDS
101 Adobe Canyon Rd. Kenwood 95452
Chardonnay,'90, Alex. Vly., Damaris Reserve $16.00 (2)
Chardonnay,'90, Sonoma, Two Williams Vnyd. $14.00 (S-State Fair)
Chardonnay,'91, Alexander Vly., Damaris Res. $16.00 (B-State Fair)
Chardonnay,'91, Sonoma Co., Overlook $12.00 (6)
Chardonnay,'91, Sonoma, Two Williams Vnyd. $14.00 (2)

LANG WINES
6060 Granite Springs Road Somerset 95684
Zinfandel,'90, Twin Rivers Vnyd. (G-L.A.)

LANGTRY
21000 Butts Canyon Rd. Middletown 95461
Red Meritage,'89, Lake Co. $35.00 (4)
Red Meritage,'90, California $35.00 (4)
White Meritage,'90, Guenoc Vly. $17.00 (2)
White Meritage,'91, Guenoc Vly. $17.00 (S-San Fran)

AS VINAS
5573 Woodbridge Rd. Lodl 95242
Cabernet Sauvignon,'90, Peltier Vnyd., Estate (S-New World)

ATCHAM VINEYARDS
Address Not Available
Cabernet Franc,'91, Sierra Foothills (G-State Fair)
Cabernet Sauvignon,'90, El Dorado $12.00 (2)
Chardonnay,'91, El Dorado $8.50 (B-Orange)
Zinfandel,'90, El Dorado $8.00 (2)

AURIER
6342 Bystrum Road Ceres 95307
Chardonnay,'89, Sonoma Co. $15.00 (4)

AVA CAP WINERY
2221 Fruitridge Rd. Placerville 95667
Cabernet Sauvignon,'89, El Dorado, Estate $13.00 (4)
Chardonnay,'91, El Dorado, Reserve $13.00 (4)
Merlot,'90, El Dorado Co., Estate $13.00 (3)
Sauvignon Blanc,'91, El Dorado Co. Fume $8.00 (B-San Diego)
Zinfandel,'90, El Dorado $9.00 (B-State Fair)

AZY CREEK VINEYARD
4610 Hwy. 128 Philo 95466
Gewurztraminer,'92, Anderson Vly. (B-State Fair)

E DOMAINE
P. O. Box 99 Madera 93639
Sparkling Wine,'NV, California, Brut $4.00 (B-Orange)

EWARD WINERY
2784 Johnson Dr. Ventura 93003
Cabernet Sauvignon,'88, Alexander Vly. $13.00 (S-Orange)
Chardonnay,'90, Monterey $14.00 (2)
Chardonnay,'91, Central Coast $11.00 (5)
Chardonnay,'91, Edna Vly., Reserve $15.00 (B-State Fair)
Merlot,'89, Napa Vly. (B-W. Coast)

BERTY SCHOOL
8700 Conn Creek Road Rutherford 94573
Chardonnay,'91, Santa Maria, Barrel Ferm. (B-New World)

MERICK LANE
1023 Limerick Lane Healdsburg 95448
Sauvignon Blanc,'92, Russian River, Collins Vnyd. $7.00 (2)
Zinfandel,'91, Russian River Vly. $12.00 (5)

PARITA
200 Las Posados Angwin 94508
Cabernet Sauvignon,'90, Napa, Howell Mtn. $35.00 (2)
Chardonnay,'91, Napa Vly., Howell Mtn. $18.00 (S-Orange)
Merlot,'90, Napa Vly., Howell Mtn. $27.00 (G-Orange)

CKWOOD VINEYARD
1044 Harkins Road Salinas 93901
Cabernet Franc,'91, Monterey (2)
Cabernet Sauvignon,'90, Monterey $10.00 (B-W. Coast)
Cabernet Sauvignon,'91, Monterey Co. $10.00 (3)
Chardonnay,'91, Monterey $8.00 (3)
Chardonnay,'91, Monterey, Estate, Reserve $14.00 (2)

Johannisberg Riesling,'91, Monterey, Estate $8.00 (B-Dallas)
Johannisberg Riesling,'91, Monterey, Estate, LH (B-Dallas)
Merlot,'91, Monterey $9.00 (2)
Semillon,'91, Monterey, Estate (S-Dallas)

J. LOHR WINERY
1000 Lenzen Ave. San Jose 95126
Cabernet Sauvignon,'89, Seven Oaks $12.00 (Σ-New World)
Cabernet Sauvignon,'90, Paso Robles, Seven Oaks $12.25 (3)
Johannisberg Riesling,'91, Monterey, "Bay Mist" $7.00 (2)
Johannisberg Riesling,'92, Monterey, "Bay Mist" $7.25 (5)

LOLONIS WINERY
2901 Road B Redwood Vly 95470
Cabernet Sauvignon,'89, Lolonis Vnyd., Res. $16.00 (B-Orange)
Chardonnay,'91, Mendocino Co., Reserve $19.00 (2)
Sauvignon Blanc,'91, Mendocino Co., Fume $8.50 (2)
Zinfandel,'90, Mendocino Co. (S-New World)

LYNFRED WINERY
Address Not Available
Chardonnay,'90, California Reserve, Barrel Ferm. (2)

M

MAACAMA CREEK
15001 Chalk Hill Rd. Healdsburg 95448
Cabernet Sauvignon,'90, Sonoma, Melim Reserve (B-Dallas)
Cabernet Sauvignon,'90, Sonoma, Melim Vnyd. $9.00 (S-Dallas)

MACAULEY VINEYARD
3291 St. Helena Hwy. St Helena 94574
Cabernet Sauvignon,'89, Napa $15.00 (B-San Fran)

MACROSTIE WINERY
17246 Woodland Ave. Sonoma 95476
Chardonnay,'91, Carneros $14.75 (3)

MADDALENA VINEYARD
737 Lamar Street Los Angeles 90031
Johannisberg Riesling,'92, Central Coast $5.00 (3)

MADRONA VINEYARDS
P. O. Box 454, Gatlin Rd. Camino 95709
Cabernet Franc,'89, El Dorado $11.00 (2)
Chardonnay,'91, El Dorado (B-State Fair)
Gewurztraminer,'92, El Dorado $7.00 (S-Orange)
Merlot,'89, El Dorado $11.00 (B-Farmers)

MAISON DEUTZ WINERY
453 Deutz Dr. Arroyo Grande 93420
Sparkling Wine,'NV, SLO/S. Barbara, Blanc de Noir $16.00 (2)
Sparkling Wine,'NV, SLO/S. Barbara, Brut Cuvee $15.00 (7)
Sparkling Wine,'NV, SLO/S. Barbara, Brut Rose $24.00 (4)

MARIETTA CELLARS
P.O. Box 1260 Healdsburg 95448
Cabernet Sauvignon,'90, Sonoma Co. $12.00 (B-Orange)

M. MARION
5350 Skylane Blvd. #201 Santa Rosa 95403
Cabernet Sauvignon,'91, Napa Vly. (2)

Chardonnay,'92, Sonoma Co. $8.00 (B-Orange)
Merlot,'91, Napa Vly. (2)
Sauvignon Blanc,'92, Sonoma Co. $7.00 (2)

MARK WEST VINEYARDS
7000 Trenton-Healdsburg Rd. Forestville 95436
Chardonnay,'91, Russian River Vly. $12.50 (B-San Diego)
Gewurztraminer,'91, Russian River Vly., Reserve (S-Dallas)

MARKHAM VINEYARDS
2812 N. St. Helena Hwy. St Helena 94574
Cabernet Sauvignon,'89, Napa Vly. $14.00 (2)
Cabernet Sauvignon,'90, Napa Vly. $8.00 (S-San Fran)
Chardonnay,'91, Napa Vly. $14.00 (B-San Fran)
Merlot,'90, Napa Vly. $15.00 (2)
Sauvignon Blanc,'91, Napa Vly. $8.00 (2)
Sauvignon Blanc,'92, Napa Vly. $8.00 (B-State Fair)

MARTINELLI VINEYARDS
3360 River Road Windsor 95436
Sauvignon Blanc,'91, Russian River Vly., Estate (S-San Diego)

LOUIS M. MARTINI WINERY
254 St. Helena Hwy., N. St Helena 94574
Cabernet Sauvignon,'89, Napa Vly., Reserve $14.00 (2)
Cabernet Sauvignon,'89, Sonoma, Monte Rosso Vnyd. $22.00 (5)
Chardonnay,'90, Napa Vly., Reserve $15.00 (B-New World)
Chardonnay,'91, Napa Vly. $8.00 (4)
Pinot Noir,'90, Napa, La Loma Vnyd. $14.00 (2)
Zinfandel,'89, Sonoma Co./Napa Co. $7.00 (2)

PAUL MASSON VINEYARDS
13150 Saratoga Ave. Saratoga 95070
Cabernet Sauvignon,'88, Monterey Co. $8.00 (3)
Chardonnay,'91, Monterey Co. $8.00 (B-San Diego)
Chardonnay,'92, Monterey, Vintners Select, Res. $5.00 (B-Orange)
Chenin Blanc,'NV, California Premium $3.00 (B-Orange)
Merlot,'91, Monterey Co. $8.00 (2)
Sauvignon Blanc,'91, Monterey, Reserve $5.00 (B-Orange)
Sparkling Wine,'88, Monterey, Grand Cuvee (B-Dallas)

MATANZAS CREEK WINERY
6097 Bennett Vly. Rd. Santa Rosa 95404
Chardonnay,'90, Sonoma Vly. $19.00 (B-Dallas)
Merlot,'90, Sonoma Vly. (S-Dallas)
Sauvignon Blanc,'91, Sonoma Co. (B-New World)

MAYA
7776 Silverado Trail Yountville 94599
Red Meritage,'89, Napa Vly. $48.00 (2)

MAZZOCCO VINEYARDS
1400 Lytton Springs Rd. Healdsburg 95448
Cabernet Sauvignon,'89, Sonoma Co. $15.00 (5)
Chardonnay,'91, Sonoma Co., River Lane $15.00 (6)
Red Meritage,'89, Sonoma, Matrix $28.00 (B-San Fran)
Zinfandel,'90, Sonoma Co. (G-Dallas)

MC DOWELL VALLEY VINEYARDS
3811 Highway 175 Hopland 95449
Syrah,'88, McDowell Vly, Les Vieux Cepages $15.95 (B-Farmers)

Syrah,'90, Les Vieux Cepages (G-L.A.)

MC HENRY VINEYARD
330 11th Street Davis 95616
Pinot Noir,'89, Santa Cruz Mtns., Estate $12.50 (G-L.A.)

MC ILROY WINES
Address Not Available
Chardonnay,'91, Russian River, Aquarious $14.50 (4)

MEEKER VINEYARD
9711 W. Dry Creek Rd. Healdsburg 95448
Cabernet Sauvignon,'90, Dry Creek Vly. $14.00 (B-W. Coast)

MENDOCINO HILLS
Address Not Available
Cabernet Sauvignon,'89, Mendocino Co. $18.00 (4)

MERIDIAN VINEYARDS
7000 Hwy. 46 East Paso Robles 93447
Cabernet Sauvignon,'90, Paso Robles $13.00 (2)
Chardonnay,'91, Edna Vly. $14.00 (5)
Chardonnay,'91, Santa Barbara Co. $10.00 (B-Farmers)
Pinot Noir,'90, Santa Barbara Co. $14.00 (5)
Sauvignon Blanc,'92, California $8.25 (2)
Syrah,'90, Paso Robles $14.00 (7)
Zinfandel,'89, Paso Robles (B-San Diego)

MARILYN MERLOT
Address Not Available
Merlot,'89, Napa Vly. $14.00 (S-Orange)

MERRY VINTNERS
3339 Hartman Rd. Santa Rosa 95401
Chardonnay,'89, Sonoma Co. $12.00 (B-Farmers)
Chardonnay,'89, Sonoma Co., Reserve $15.00 (S-Farmers)

MERRYVALE VINEYARDS
3640 Buchanan St. San Francisco 94123
Cabernet Sauvignon,'90, Napa Vly. (S-State Fair)
Chardonnay,'91, Napa Vly., Starmont $16.00 (2)
Red Meritage,'88, Napa Vly., Profile $30.00 (S-Dallas)
Red Meritage,'89, Napa Vly., Profile $30.00 (4)
White Meritage,'92, Napa Vly. $13.00 (3)

PETER MICHAEL WINERY
12400 Ida Clayton Rd. Calistoga 94515
Cabernet Sauvignon,'89, Les Pavots $26.00 (B-Orange)

MILL CREEK VINEYARDS
1401 Westside Rd. Healdsburg 95448
Cabernet Sauvignon,'90, Dry Creek Vly., Reserve (B-State Fair)
Chardonnay,'92, Dry Creek Vly. (S-State Fair)
Gewurztraminer,'92, Dry Creek Vly., Estate (2)
Merlot,'89, Dry Creek, Estate $12.00 (4)
Sauvignon Blanc,'92, Dry Creek (G-W. Coast)

MIRABELLE
Address Not Available
Sparkling Wine,'NV, Brut $8.75 (S-Orange)

MIRASSOU VINEYARDS
3000 Aborn Rd. San Jose 95135

Cabernet Sauvignon,'90, Monterey Co., Reserve $12.00 (3)
Cabernet Sauvignon,'90, Monterey, Fam. Sel. $9.75 (B-State Fair)
Chardonnay,'90, Monterey, Harvest Reserve $12.50 (2)
Chardonnay,'91, Monterey, Family Selection $9.75 (4)
Chardonnay,'91, Monterey, Harvest Reserve $12.50 (3)
Chenin Blanc,'91, Monterey $6.50 (2)
Chenin Blanc,'92, Monterey, Family Sel. $6.50 (B-State Fair)
Johannisberg Riesling,'87, Monterey, LH (G-W. Coast)
Merlot,'91, Monterey Co., Family Sel. $9.00 (3)
Petite Sirah,'90, Monterey, Family Selection $7.50 (B-Farmers)
Pinot Blanc,'90, Monterey Co., Harvest Reserve $12.00 (2)
Pinot Blanc,'91, Monterey Co., Harvest Reserve $13.00 (5)
Pinot Blanc,'91, Monterey, Family Sel., Wt. Burgundy $7.50 (6)
Pinot Blanc,'92, Monterey, Family Selection $7.00 (2)
Pinot Noir,'89, Monterey, Harvest Reserve $13.00 (2)
Pinot Noir,'90, Monterey Co., Family Selection $7.50 (B-New World)
Pinot Noir,'90, Monterey Co., Harvest Reserve (B-State Fair)
Sauvignon Blanc,'91, California $5.00 (2)
Sparkling Wine,'85, Monterey Co., Reserve, Brut $15.00 (5)
Sparkling Wine,'88, Monterey, Brut Reserve $15.00 (S-San Fran)
Sparkling Wine,'89, Monterey Co. Au Natural $13.00 (6)
Sparkling Wine,'89, Monterey, Brut $13.00 (B-Dallas)
Sparkling Wine,'90, Monterey, Blanc de Noirs $13.00 (7)
Sparkling Wine,'90, Monterey, Brut $13.00 (5)
White Zinfandel,'92, California $5.50 (S-W. Coast)

MISSION VIEW ESTATE
P. O. Box 129 San Miguel 93451

Cabernet Sauvignon,'89, Paso Robles $12.00 (B-State Fair)
Pinot Noir,'90, Monterey Co., Ltd. Release (G-New World)

C. K. MONDAVI
2800 St. Helena Hwy. St Helena 94574

Chardonnay,'92, California $5.75 (S-Orange)

ROBERT MONDAVI WINERY
7801 St. Helena Hwy. Oakville 94562

Cabernet Sauvignon,'89, Napa Vly. $18.00 (G-New World)
Cabernet Sauvignon,'89, Napa Vly., Reserve $40.00 (B-Orange)
Chardonnay,'90, Napa Vly. $13.00 (B-New World)
Chardonnay,'91, Napa Vly. $13.00 (B-San Fran)
Johannisberg Riesling,'83, Napa Vly., Botrytis, LH $37.00 (S-Orange)
Merlot,'90, Napa Vly. (S-New World)
Pinot Noir,'91, Napa Vly., Reserve $24.50 (B-Orange)
Pinot Noir,'91, Napa Vly., Unfiltered $13.00 (2)

MONT ST. JOHN CELLARS
5400 Old Sonoma Rd. Napa 94558

Gewurztraminer,'92, Napa Vly., Carneros, Estate $6.75 (S-Orange)
Pinot Noir,'89, Carneros, Madonna Vnyd. $16.00 (B-Orange)
Pinot Noir,'90, Carneros, Madonna Vnyd. $16.00 (G-Dallas)

MONTEREY PENINSULA WINERY
467 Shasta Ave. Sand City 93955

Cabernet Sauvignon,'85, Monterey Co. $12.00 (S-Orange)
Merlot,'87, Monterey, Dr's Reserve (2)

MONTEREY VINEYARD
800 So. Alta St. Gonzales 93926
Cabernet Sauvignon,'90, Monterey Co., Classic (G-New World)
Cabernet Sauvignon,'91, Monterey Co., Classic $6.00 (3)
Chardonnay,'89, Ltd. Release (B-L.A.)
Chardonnay,'91, Monterey Co., Classic (S-New World)
Merlot,'91, Monterey/Napa Co. $6.00 (B-Farmers)
White Zinfandel,'92, Monterey Co. Classic $5.00 (2)

MONTEVINA WINES
20680 Shenandoah School Plymouth 95669
Cabernet Sauvignon,'90, California (2)
Sauvignon Blanc,'91, California, Fume $6.50 (3)
White Zinfandel,'92, Amador Co. (B-State Fair)

MONTICELLO CELLARS
4242 Big Ranch Rd. Napa 94558
Cabernet Sauvignon,'89, Napa Vly., Corley Reserve $25.00 (5)
Cabernet Sauvignon,'89, Napa Vly., Select $18.00 (B-Orange)
Chardonnay,'90, Napa Vly., Corley Reserve $25.00 (S-L.A.)
Merlot,'90, Napa Vly., Estate $18.00 (S-San Fran)
Pinot Noir,'90, Napa Vly., Estate $18.00 (2)

MONTPELLIER VINEYARDS
P. O. Box 789 Ceres 95307
Cabernet Sauvignon,'90, California $8.00 (2)
White Zinfandel,'92, California (4)

MORGAN
526-E Brunken Avenue Salinas 93901
Cabernet Sauvignon,'89, Carmel Vly. $18.00 (2)
Chardonnay,'91, Monterey, Reserve $23.00 (2)
Pinot Noir,'91, California $15.00 (2)
Pinot Noir,'91, Monterey Co., Reserve (B-State Fair)
Pinot Noir,'91, Napa, Carneros, Reserve (B-State Fair)

J. W. MORRIS WINERY
101 Grant Ave. Healdsburg 95448
Chardonnay,'91, California, Reserve $7.00 (B-Orange)
Sauvignon Blanc,'91, California, Reserve $6.50 (B-W. Coast)

MOSBY
P. O. Box 1849 Buellton 93424
Gewurztraminer,'91, Santa Barbara, Barrel Ferm. $8.00 (2)

MOSHIN VINEYARDS
Address Not Available
Pinot Noir,'91, Russian River, Sp. Barrel Sel. $25.00 (S-San Fran)

MOSS CREEK WINERY
6015 Steele Canyon Rd. Napa 94558
Cabernet Sauvignon,'89, Napa Vly. (B-W. Coast)
Sauvignon Blanc,'91, Lake Co. (B-W. Coast)

MOUNT PALOMAR WINERY
33820 Rancho Calif. Rd. Temecula 92390
Chardonnay,'91, Temecula $11.00 (Σ-Farmers)
Johannisberg Riesling,'92, Temecula $6.00 (B-San Diego)
Sauvignon Blanc,'92, Temecula $8.00 (S-New World)

MOUNT VEEDER WINERY
1999 Mt. Veeder Rd. Napa 94558
Cabernet Sauvignon,'89, Napa Vly. $21.50 (4)
Chardonnay,'91, Napa Vly. $17.00 (2)
Red Meritage,'89, Napa Vly. $24.00 (7)

MOUNTAIN VIEW
2003 El Camino Real Mountain View 94040
Pinot Noir,'91, Monterey/Napa (S-New World)

MT. MADONNA
1480 E. Main Avenue Morgan Hill 95037
Chardonnay,'92, Monterey Co. (S-State Fair)
Merlot,'91, Napa Vly. $8.75 (B-Orange)

MUMM CUVEE NAPA
1111 Dunaweal Ln. Calistoga 94515
Sparkling Wine,'89, Carneros, Winery Lake Brut $18.00 (5)
Sparkling Wine,'NV, Napa Vly., Blanc de Noirs $14.00 (9)
Sparkling Wine,'NV, Napa Vly., Brut Prestige $14.00 (7)

MURPHY-GOODE WINERY
3740 Hwy. 128 Geyserville 95441
Cabernet Sauvignon,'89, Murphy Ranch $15.00 (G-San Diego)
Cabernet Sauvignon,'90, Alexander Vly., Murphy Ranch $15.00 (4)
Chardonnay,'91, Alexander Vly., Estate $12.50 (3)
Merlot,'91, (Σ-L.A.)
Sauvignon Blanc,'91, Alexander Vly., Reserve Fume (B-Dallas)
Sauvignon Blanc,'92, Alexander Vly., Fume $9.50 (5)

N

NALLE
P. O. Box 454 Healdsburg 95448
Zinfandel,'91, Dry Creek Vly. $22.00 (B-Orange)

NAPA CREEK WINERY
1001 Silverado Trail St Helena 94574
Chardonnay,'90, Napa Vly., Investor Reserve (B-State Fair)

NAPA RIDGE
P. O. Box 111 St Helena 94574
Cabernet Sauvignon,'89, North Coast, Reserve $12.00 (6)
Cabernet Sauvignon,'90, Central Coast $7.50 (2)
Cabernet Sauvignon,'91, North Coast $7.50 (B-L.A.)
Chardonnay,'91, North Coast, Reserve $12.00 (4)
Chardonnay,'91, Central Coast, Coastal Vines (2)
Chenin Blanc,'91, Central Coast $5.75 (2)
Gewurztraminer,'91, Central Coast $7.50 (2)
Pinot Noir,'91, North Coast $7.50 (4)
Sauvignon Blanc,'91, North Coast $7.50 (4)
White Zinfandel,'92, Lodi $6.00 (2)

NAPA VALLEY CHAMPAGNE CELLARS
Address Not Available
Sparkling Wine,'88, California, Blanc de Noirs (G-New World)
Sparkling Wine,'88, California, La Crema Noir (B-New World)

NAPA VILLAGES
5225 Solano Avenue Napa 94558
Pinot Noir,'90, Napa Vly. $9.00 (B-Orange)

NAVARRO VINEYARDS
5601 Highway 128 Philo 95466
Cabernet Franc,'89, Mendocino $16.00 (3)
Cabernet Sauvignon,'88, Mendocino $16.00 (4)
Chardonnay,'89, Anderson Vly., Reserve $16.00 (2)
Chardonnay,'90, Anderson Vly., Premiere Res. $16.00 (S-New World)
Chardonnay,'90, Mendocino $11.00 (2)
Chardonnay,'91, Anderson Vly., Res. $16.00 (B-State Fair)
Chardonnay,'91, Mendocino $11.00 (4)
Gewurztraminer,'91, Anderson Vly., Cuvee $8.50 (5)
Gewurztraminer,'91, North Coast, LH $12.00 (6)
Johannisberg Riesling,'89, Anderson Vly., LHCS (B-L.A.)
Johannisberg Riesling,'90, Anderson Vly., LHCS $29.00 (4)
Johannisberg Riesling,'91, Anderson Vly. $8.50 (3)
Johannisberg Riesling,'91, Deep-end Dry $12.00 (G-San Fran)
Johannisberg Riesling,'92, Anderson Vly. $9.00 (2)
Pinot Noir,'89, Anderson Vly. $15.00 (S-Farmers)
Pinot Noir,'89, Anderson Vly., Deep End Blend $18.00 (S-Farmers)
Pinot Noir,'90, Anderson Vly., A'Lancienne $15.00 (4)
Pinot Noir,'NV, Mendocino $9.00 (3)
Red Meritage,'NV, Mendocino, Navarrouge (2)
Sauvignon Blanc,'91, Mendocino, Cuvee 128 $9.75 (2)
Sparkling Wine,'88, Mendocino, Brut $16.50 (4)
Zinfandel,'91, Mendocino $14.00 (3)

NEVADA CITY WINERY
321 Spring St. Nevada City 95959
Cabernet Franc,'90, Sierra Foothills (S-W. Coast)
Cabernet Franc,'NV, Sierra Foothills $12.00 (3)
Chardonnay,'91, Nevada Co. (B-State Fair)
Gewurztraminer,'91, Sonoma Co. (G-State Fair)
Merlot,'90, Sierra Foothills $14.00 (3)
Red Meritage,'90, Sierra Foothills, Director's Reserve $14.00 (3)
Zinfandel,'91, Sierra Foothills $9.00 (2)

NEWLAN VINEYARDS
1305 Carrell Lane Napa 94558
Cabernet Sauvignon,'87, Napa Vly. $15.00 (3)
Chardonnay,'91, Napa Vly. $14.00 (4)
Johannisberg Riesling,'91, Napa Vly., LH (2)
Pinot Noir,'89, Napa Vly. $18.00 (2)
Pinot Noir,'90, Napa Vly. $18.00 (B-W. Coast)

NEWTON VINEYARD
2555 Madrona Ave. St Helena 94574
Chardonnay,'91, Napa Vly. $16.00 (S-State Fair)
Red Meritage,'91, Napa Vly., Claret $12.00 (B-Orange)

NICHELINI WINERY
2950 Sage Canyon Rd. St Helena 94574
Cabernet Sauvignon,'88, Napa Vly. (B-W. Coast)

GUSTAVE NIEBAUM COLLECTION
P. O. Box 402 Rutherford 94573
Chardonnay,'90, Bayview Vnyd., Res. $13.50 (B-State Fair)
Chardonnay,'91, Napa Vly., "Reference" $9.50 (B-Orange)

O

OAK FALLS
Address Not Available
Sparkling Wine,'NV, California, Brut (B-State Fair)

OAKVILLE BENCH CELLARS
Address Not Available
Cabernet Sauvignon,'89, Napa Vly. $12.00 (S-Farmers)
Chardonnay,'89, Napa Vly. $10.00 (Σ-Farmers)

OAKVILLE RANCH VINEYARDS
Address Not Available
Cabernet Sauvignon,'89, Napa $22.00 (G-San Fran)
Cabernet Sauvignon,'90, Napa Vly. $27.00 (2)
Chardonnay,'91, Napa $18.00 (B-San Fran)
Chardonnay,'91, Napa, Vista $18.00 (S-San Fran)

OBESTER WINERY
12341 San Mateo Rd. Half Moon Bay 94019
Chardonnay,'90, Mendocino Co., Barrel Ferm. (3)
Sauvignon Blanc,'91, Mendocino Co. $9.00 (4)
Zinfandel,'90, Mendocino $16.00 (S-San Fran)

OJAI VINEYARDS
P. O. Box 952 Oakview 93022
White Meritage,'91, Ste. Helene, Res. $15.00 (B-Orange)

OLIVET LANE ESTATE
P. O. Box 2386 So San Francisco 94083
Chardonnay,'91, Russian River Vly. $11.00 (2)
Pinot Noir,'91, Russian River Vly. $11.00 (B-Orange)

ONE VINEYARD
3291 St. Helena Hwy. St Helena 94574
Cabernet Sauvignon,'89, Ehlers Lane Vnyds. (B-State Fair)

OPUS ONE
7900 St. Helena Hwy. Oakville 94562
Red Meritage,'89, Napa Vly. $69.00 (B-Orange)

P

PACHECO RANCH WINERY
5495 Redwood Hwy. Ignacio 94947
Cabernet Sauvignon,'86, Pacheco Vnyds. $12.00 (S-San Diego)
Cabernet Sauvignon,'87, Marin Co., Estate $12.00 (B-Farmers)

PAHLMEYER
P. O. Box 2410 Napa 94558
Red Meritage,'89, Napa, Caldwell Vnyd. $32.00 (G-Orange)

PARAISO SPRINGS VINEYARDS
38060 Paraiso Springs Rd. Soledad 93960
Chardonnay,'91, Monterey (2)
Johannisberg Riesling,'91, Monterey $6.00 (S-San Fran)
Pinot Blanc,'91, Monterey Co. $8.00 (2)

PARDUCCI WINE CELLARS
501 Parducci Rd. Ukiah 95482
Cabernet Franc,'89, Mendocino Co. $9.50 (B-State Fair)
Chenin Blanc,'92, Mendocino Co. $6.00 (4)

Gewurztraminer,'92, Mendocino Co. $7.25 (3)
Petite Sirah,'89, Mendocino Co. $6.00 (2)
Petite Sirah,'90, Mendocino Co. $6.99 (B-State Fair)
Pinot Noir,'90, Mendocino $7.00 (2)
Pinot Noir,'91, Mendocino Co. $7.00 (B-Orange)
Sauvignon Blanc,'92, Mendocino Co. $6.00 (S-Orange)
Zinfandel,'90, Mendocino $7.00 (3)
Zinfandel,'91, Mendocino Co. $7.00 (B-State Fair)

PEACHY CANYON WINERY
Rt. 1, Box 115C Paso Robles 93446
Zinfandel,'90, Paso Robles, Especial $14.00 (G-San Fran)
Zinfandel,'91, Paso Robles, Westside $12.00 (S-San Fran)

J. PEDRONCELLI WINERY
1220 Canyon Rd. Geyserville 95441
Cabernet Sauvignon,'86, Dry Creek Vly., Reserve $14.00 (3)
Chardonnay,'91, Dry Creek Vly. $9.00 (2)
Johannisberg Riesling,'90, Dry Creek Vly., Estate $5.50 (B-Orange)
Merlot,'90, Dry Creek Vly. $10.00 (B-Orange)
Pinot Noir,'90, Dry Creek Vly. $9.00 (2)
Sauvignon Blanc,'91, Dry Creek Vly., Fume $8.00 (2)
White Zinfandel,'92, Sonoma Co. Rose $5.50 (3)
Zinfandel,'90, (B-L.A.)

PEJU PROVINCE
8466 St. Helena Hwy. Rutherford 94573
Cabernet Sauvignon,'89, Napa Vly., HB Vnyd. $30.00 (3)
Cabernet Sauvignon,'90, Napa Vly. $15.00 (B-W. Coast)
Cabernet Sauvignon,'90, Napa Vly., HB Vnyd. $30.00 (2)
Chardonnay,'91, Napa Vly. $15.00 (S-San Fran)

PELLEGRINI FAMILY VINEYARDS
272 So. Maple Ave. So San Francisco 94080
Cabernet Sauvignon,'89, Cloverdale Ranch (S-State Fair)

PENARD
Address Not Available
Chardonnay,'91, Carneros $19.00 (2)

ROBERT PEPI WINERY
7585 St. Helena Hwy. Oakville 94562
Chardonnay,'90, Napa Vly., Puncheon Ferm. $16.00 (B-Farmers)
Chardonnay,'91, Napa Vly., Puncheon Ferm. $16.00 (B-San Diego)
Sauvignon Blanc,'91, Napa Vly., Reserve Sel. $18.00 (4)
Sauvignon Blanc,'91, Two-Heart Canopy $9.50 (B-Orange)
White Meritage,'91, Napa Vly., Two-Heart Canopy (S-San Diego)

MARIO PERELLI-MINETTI
1443 Silverado Trail St Helena 94574
Cabernet Sauvignon,'89, Napa Vly. $12.50 (B-Orange)

PERRY CREEK VINEYARDS
Address Not Available
Cabernet Franc,'90, El Dorado $11.50 (3)
Cabernet Sauvignon,'90, El Dorado Co. (3)
Chardonnay,'92, El Dorado (B-State Fair)
White Zinfandel,'92, El Dorado (B-State Fair)
Zinfandel,'90, El Dorado Co. $8.00 (6)
Zinfandel,'92, El Dorado Co. $8.00 (3)

ESENTI WINVERY
2900 Vineyard Dr. Templeton 93465
Johannisberg Riesling,'NV, Shandon Vly. Vnyd. (G-L.A.)
Zinfandel,'90, Paso Robles, Dry LH (B-L.A.)

OSEPH PHELPS VINEYARDS
200 Taplin Road St Helena 94574
Cabernet Sauvignon,'88, Napa Vly., Insignia $18.00 (G-State Fair)
Cabernet Sauvignon,'89, Napa Vly., Insignia $18.00 (B-Dallas)
Cabernet Sauvignon,'90, Napa Vly. $18.00 (2)
Chardonnay,'91, Napa Vly. (3)
Merlot,'90, Napa Vly. $16.00 (2)
Red Meritage,'88, Napa Vly., Insignia (G-L.A.)
Syrah,'90, Napa Vly. $16.00 (B-Orange)

R. H. PHILLIP VINEYARD
Route 1, Box 855 Esparto 95627
Cabernet Sauvignon,'91, California $8.00 (2)
Chardonnay,'91, California, Barrel Cuvee $8.00 (S-New World)
Chardonnay,'92, California, Barrel Cuvee $8.00 (4)

. H. PHILLIP VINEYARD
Route 1, Box 855 Esparto 95627
Chenin Blanc,'91, California $5.00 (2)

R. H. PHILLIP VINEYARD
Route 1, Box 855 Esparto 95627
Chenin Blanc,'92, California $5.00 (3)
Sauvignon Blanc,'92, California $6.00 (3)
Syrah,'89, California, EXP (3)
White Zinfandel,'92, California $5.00 (3)

INE RIDGE WINERY
5901 Silverado Trail Napa 94558
Cabernet Sauvignon,'91, Stags Leap Dist. (B-L.A.)
Chardonnay,'90, Napa Vly., Stags Leap Dist. $20.00 (B-Orange)
Chenin Blanc,'92, Napa Vly., Yountville Cuvee $7.50 (B-Orange)
Merlot,'90, Napa Vly., Selected Cuvee $17.50 (S-Orange)

INNACLES ESTATE
P. O. Box 407 Rutherford 94573
Chardonnay,'91, Monterey Co. (3)
Pinot Noir,'90, Monterey (G-Dallas)
Pinot Noir,'91, Monterey, Pinnacles Vnyd. (S-State Fair)

PER SONOMA
11447 Old Redwood Hwy. Healdsburg 95448
Sparkling Wine,'88, Sonoma Co., Brut $14.00 (B-Orange)

OPPY HILL
Address Not Available
Merlot,'90, Napa Vly., Founder's Selection (S-Dallas)

ORTER CREEK VINEYARDS
8735 Westside Rd. Healdsburg 95448
Chardonnay,'92, Russian River Vly. (S-State Fair)

RNARD PRADEL CELLARS
2100 Hoffman Lane Yountville 94599
Cabernet Sauvignon,'89, Napa Vly., Ltd. Barrel Sel. (B-San Diego)

PRESTON VINEYARDS

9282 W. Dry Creek Rd. Healdsburg 95448

Cabernet Sauvignon,'89, Dry Creek Vly. $14.00 (G-L.A.)
Chenin Blanc,'91, Dry Creek Vly., Estate $7.00 (2)
Sauvignon Blanc,'91, Cuvee de Fume $8.00 (S-San Fran)
Zinfandel,'90, Dry Creek Vly. (2)

Q

QUAIL RIDGE CELLARS

1055 Atlas Peak Road Napa 94558

Chardonnay,'90, Napa Vly. $15.00 (4)
Merlot,'89, Napa Vly. $15.00 (2)
Sauvignon Blanc,'91, Napa Vly. $8.00 (3)

QUIVIRA VINEYARDS

4900 W. Dry Creek Rd. Healdsburg 95448

Red Meritage,'89, Dry Creek Vly.,Cuvee (2)
Sauvignon Blanc,'91, Dry Creek Vly. $10.00 (B-Dallas)
Zinfandel,'91, Dry Creek Vly. $13.25 (3)

QUPE CELLARS

2440 Lucca Ave. Los Olivos 93441

Syrah,'91, Santa Barbara, Bien Nacido, Res. $20.00 (B-Orange)

R

RABBIT RIDGE VINEYARDS

3291 Westside Rd. Healdsburg 95448

Cabernet Sauvignon,'89, Sonoma Co. $12.00 (G-Orange)
Chardonnay,'91, Russian River Vly. $16.00 (3)
Petite Sirah,'90, Sonoma Co. $9.50 (4)
White Meritage,'91, Sonoma Co., Mystique $7.00 (2)
Zinfandel,'91, Dry Creek Vly. $9.50 (6)
Zinfandel,'91, Sonoma, San Lorenzo Vnyd., Res. $14.00 (G-Orange)

RADANOVICH VINEYARDS

3936 Ben Hur Road Mariposa 95338

Merlot,'91, Sierra Foothills (B-State Fair)

A. RAFANELLI WINERY

4685 West Dry Creek Rd. Healdsburg 95448

Cabernet Sauvignon,'90, Dry Creek Vly., Unfiltered $15.00 (5)
Zinfandel,'91, Dry Creek Vly. $11.75 (4)

RAMSEY

2125 Cuttings Wharf Rd. Napa 94559

Syrah,'91, Napa Vly. $9.00 (B-Farmers)

RANCHO SISQUOC

Rt. 1, Box 147 Santa Maria 93454

Cabernet Sauvignon,'89, Santa Maria Vly. $14.00 (2)
Chardonnay,'91, Santa Maria Vly., Estate $14.00 (2)
Merlot,'91, Santa Maria Vly., Estate $13.00 (B-Orange)
Red Meritage,'89, Santa Maria Vly., Cellar Sel. $25.00 (2)

KENT RASMUSSEN WINERY

2125 Cuttings Wharf Rd. Napa 94559

Chardonnay,'91, Napa Vly. $17.00 (B-Farmers)
Pinot Noir,'90, Carneros $18.00 (B-Dallas)
Syrah,'91, Napa Vly. (S-W. Coast)

RAVENSWOOD

21415 Broadway   Sonoma   95476

Merlot,'90, Sonoma Co. $15.00 (2)
Merlot,'91, North Coast, Vintner's Blend $10.00 (B-Orange)
Red Meritage,'90, Sonoma Mtn., Pickberry $26.00 (S-Orange)
Zinfandel,'91, North Coast, Vintner's Blend $7.75 (G-Orange)

RAYMOND VINEYARD

849 Zinfandel Lane   St Helena   94574

Cabernet Sauvignon,'87, Napa Vly., Reserve $25.00 (3)
Cabernet Sauvignon,'88, Napa Vly., Reserve $25.00 (2)
Cabernet Sauvignon,'89, Napa Vly. $15.00 (4)
Cabernet Sauvignon,'90, Napa Vly. $15.00 (G-L.A.)
Chardonnay,'90, Napa Vly. $13.00 (3)
Chardonnay,'91, California $9.00 (B-State Fair)
Chardonnay,'91, Napa Vly. $13.00 (B-State Fair)
Chardonnay,'91, Napa Vly., Reserve $17.00 (4)
Sauvignon Blanc,'91, Napa Vly. $10.00 (G-Dallas)
Semillon,'89, Napa Vly., SLH   (B-State Fair)

RED ROCK WINERY

Address Not Available

Zinfandel,'89, California $8.00 (3)

RENAISSANCE VINEYARD

P. O. Box 1000   Renaissance   95962

Cabernet Sauvignon,'87, North Yuba, Estate $15.00 (G-San Diego)
Cabernet Sauvignon,'88, North Yuba, Estate $15.00 (B-San Diego)
Johannisberg Riesling,'85, North Yuba, SSLH $25.00 (B-San Diego)
Johannisberg Riesling,'88, North Yuba, SLH $25.00 (G-State Fair)
Johannisberg Riesling,'90, North Yuba, Estate $8.00 (2)
Sauvignon Blanc,'90, North Yuba $10.00 (S-W. Coast)
Sauvignon Blanc,'90, North Yuba, LH $14.00 (S-State Fair)

RETZLAFF VINEYARDS

1356 So. Livermore Ave.   Livermore   94550

Cabernet Sauvignon,'91, Livermore Vly.   (B-San Diego)

RICHARDSON VINEYARDS

2711 Knob Hill Rd.   Sonoma   95476

Cabernet Sauvignon,'90, Sonoma Vly. $14.00 (S-W. Coast)
Merlot,'91, Sangiacomo/Gregory Vnyds. $15.00 (2)
Merlot,'91, Sonoma Vly., Carneros, Gregory $18.00 (S-Orange)
Pinot Noir,'91, Los Carneros, Sonoma Vly. $15.00 (2)

RIVER RUN

65 Rogge Lane   Watsonville   95076

Johannisberg Riesling,'92, Monterey Co. $7.00 (2)
Syrah,'91, Monterey Co., Ventana Vnyd. $11.00 (4)
Zinfandel,'92, California, LH $9.00 (2)

ROCHIOLI VINEYARD

6192 Westside Road   Healdsburg   95448

Chardonnay,'91, Russian River $15.00 (3)
Gewurztraminer,'92, Russian River, McIlroy Vnyd.   (G-San Diego)
Pinot Noir,'91, Russian River Vly., Estate $18.00 (4)
Sauvignon Blanc,'91, Russian River Vly., Estate, LH   (B-San Diego)
Sauvignon Blanc,'92, Russian River Vly., Estate $11.00 (6)

ROEDERER ESTATE
4501 Highway 128 Philo 95466
Sparkling Wine,'NV, Anderson Vly., Estate, Brut $15.00 (B-Orange)

ROMBAUER VINEYARDS
3522 Silverado Trail St Helena 94574
Cabernet Sauvignon,'88, Napa Vly., Vintage $15.00 (B-Dallas)
Chardonnay,'90, Napa Vly., Reserve $20.00 (2)
Chardonnay,'91, Carneros $15.00 (4)
Red Meritage,'87, Napa, Le Meilleur Du Chai $35.00 (4)

ROSENBLUM CELLARS
2900 Main Street Alameda 94501
Cabernet Sauvignon,'90, George Hendry Vnyd. (B-State Fair)
Cabernet Sauvignon,'90, Napa Vly. (B-W. Coast)
Petite Sirah,'90, Napa Vly., Palisades Vnyds. (S-Dallas)
Petite Sirah,'91, Napa Vly. $12.00 (4)
Pinot Noir,'91, Russian River Vly., Ellis Ranch $10.50 (B-Farmers)
Red Meritage,'91, Holbrook Mitchell Trio $22.00 (B-Orange)
Red Meritage,'91, Napa Vly. $22.00 (Σ-W. Coast)
Semillon,'92, Sonoma Co., Sem-Chard $8.25 (S-Farmers)
Zinfandel,'91, Contra Costa Co. $10.00 (S-New World)
Zinfandel,'91, Mt. Veeder, Brandlin Ranch $16.00 (2)
Zinfandel,'91, Paso Robles, Richard Sauret $10.50 (2)
Zinfandel,'91, Samsel Vnyd., Maggie's Res. $16.50 (B-Orange)
Zinfandel,'91, Sonoma Co. $11.50 (2)
Zinfandel,'NV, California, Vintner's Cuvee VI $7.50 (2)

ROUDON-SMITH VINEYARDS
2364 Bean Creek Rd. Santa Cruz 95066
Cabernet Sauvignon,'91, California $10.00 (S-San Fran)
Gewurztraminer,'92, Santa Cruz Co. $8.00 (B-Orange)

ROUND HILL CELLARS
1680 Silverado Trail St Helena 94574
Cabernet Sauvignon,'87, Napa, Library $15.00 (B-San Fran)
Cabernet Sauvignon,'89, California $7.00 (B-W. Coast)
Cabernet Sauvignon,'89, Napa Vly. $11.00 (B-State Fair)
Chardonnay,'90, Napa Vly., Reserve $11.00 (B-New World)
Chardonnay,'91, Napa Vly., Reserve $11.00 (3)
Gewurztraminer,'92, California $7.00 (B-Orange)
Merlot,'90, Napa Vly., Reserve $11.00 (2)
Red Meritage,'89, Napa, Quintessence $15.00 (B-San Fran)
Sauvignon Blanc,'91, California Fume $5.00 (B-Orange)
Sauvignon Blanc,'91, Napa Vly. Fume $7.00 (S-Orange)
Zinfandel,'90, Napa Vly. $7.00 (5)

ROYCE VINEYARDS
1138 Apple Creek Ln. Santa Rosa 95401
Cabernet Sauvignon,'89, Napa Vly. (3)
Chardonnay,'91, California (2)
Chardonnay,'91, Mendocino, Reserve $17.00 (B-Orange)
Merlot,'91, Sonoma Co. (3)
White Zinfandel,'92, Mendocino (S-State Fair)

RSV
6320 Silverado Trail Napa 94558
Red Meritage,'89, Carneros Claret $28.00 (B-Orange)

RUBISSOW-SARGENT WINE CO.
Address Not Available
Merlot,'89, Mt. Veeder $15.00 (Σ-San Fran)

RUTHERFORD ESTATE CELLARS
P. O. Box 402 Rutherford 94573
Cabernet Sauvignon,'90, Napa Vly. (B-State Fair)
Chardonnay,'91, Napa Vly. $7.00 (2)
Merlot,'90, Napa Vly., Reserve $9.00 (S-Orange)

RUTHERFORD HILL WINERY
200 Rutherford Hill Rd. Rutherford 94573
Cabernet Sauvignon,'84, Napa, Library Reserve $23.00 (2)
Cabernet Sauvignon,'86, Napa, XVS Reserve $23.00 (B-San Fran)
Cabernet Sauvignon,'87, Napa Vly. $14.00 (S-Farmers)
Cabernet Sauvignon,'87, Napa Vly., XVS $23.00 (B-Farmers)
Cabernet Sauvignon,'88, (S-L.A.)
Chardonnay,'89, Napa Vly., XVS $18.00 (5)
Chardonnay,'90, Napa Vly., Jaeger Vnyds. $12.00 (2)
Merlot,'89, Napa Vly. $14.00 (2)
Sauvignon Blanc,'90, Napa Vly. $10.00 (S-Farmers)

RUTHERFORD RANCH
1680 Silverado Trail St Helena 94574
Merlot,'91, Napa Vly $9.00 (S-Orange)

S

SADDLE GROVE
Address Not Available
Chardonnay,'91, California (S-State Fair)

SAINTSBURY WINERY
1500 Los Carneros Ave. Napa 94558
Pinot Noir,'91, Carneros $16.50 (B-Orange)
Pinot Noir,'91, Carneros, Garnet $10.00 (B-Orange)

SALAMANDRE WINE CELLARS
108 Don Carlos Drive Aptos 95003
Chardonnay,'91, Arroyo Seco $14.00 (B-Orange)
Merlot,'91, Arroyo Seco $14.00 (2)

SAN MARTIN
12900 Monterey Rd. San Martin 95046
White Zinfandel,'92, California (B-W. Coast)

SANFORD WINERY
7250 Santa Rosa Rd. Buelton 93427
Chardonnay,'91, Santa Barbara Co. (B-W. Coast)
Pinot Noir,'91, Santa Barbara Co. $16.00 (2)
Sauvignon Blanc,'91, Santa Barbara Co. (2)

SANTA BARBARA WINERY
202 Anacapa St. Santa Barbara 93101
Cabernet Sauvignon,'89, Santa Ynez Vly. $10.50 (B-W. Coast)
Cabernet Sauvignon,'90, Santa Ynez Vly. $10.50 (B-Orange)
Chardonnay,'90, Santa Barbara Co. $12.00 (B-New World)
Chardonnay,'90, Santa Barbara Co., Reserve $20.00 (3)
Chenin Blanc,'90, Santa Ynez Vly. Barrel Ferm. $8.00 (2)
Johannisberg Riesling,'92, Santa Barbara Co. $8.50 (4)
Sauvignon Blanc,'90, Santa Ynez Vly., Reserve (B-Dallas)

Zinfandel,'90, (B-L.A.)
Zinfandel,'92, Santa Ynez Vly., Beaujour $9.00 (3)

SANTA YNEZ WINERY

P. O. Box 558 Santa Ynez 93460

Sauvignon Blanc,'92, California $7.00 (B-Orange)

SANTINO WINES

Rt. 2, Box 21-A Plymouth 95669

Johannisberg Riesling,'89, Sonoma Co., DBSH $18.00 (2)
Sauvignon Blanc,'89, Le Lou-Bricant, SLH $18.00 (2)
White Zinfandel,'89, Amador, DBS White Harvest $14.00 (2)
White Zinfandel,'92, Amador Co., White Harvest $6.00 (3)
Zinfandel,'89, Amador Co., Aged Release $8.00 (2)
Zinfandel,'89, Amador Co., White Harvest, LH $14.00 (2)
Zinfandel,'89, Shenandoah Vly., Grandpere $12.00 (4)
Zinfandel,'90, Amador Co., Aged Release $8.00 (B-Orange)
Zinfandel,'NV, Amador Co., Alfresco $6.00 (3)

V. SATTUI WINERY

1111 White Lane St Helena 94574

Cabernet Franc,'90, Napa Vly., Rosen Brand Vnyd. (2)
Cabernet Sauvignon,'88, Napa Vly. $14.75 (4)
Cabernet Sauvignon,'88, Napa Vly., Preston, Reserve $35.00 (3)
Cabernet Sauvignon,'89, Napa Vly., Suzanne's Vnyd. $15.00 (3)
Chardonnay,'91, Napa Vly., Carsi Vnyd., Estate $16.00 (5)
Johannisberg Riesling,'92, Napa Vly. $9.50 (7)
Johannisberg Riesling,'92, Napa Vly., Off Dry $10.00 (5)
Sauvignon Blanc,'92, Suzanne's Vnyd., Estate (2)
White Zinfandel,'92, California $7.50 (3)
Zinfandel,'90, Napa Vly., Suzanne's Vnyd. $12.75 (2)

SAUCELITO CANYON

1600 Saucelito Creek Rd. Arroyo Grande 93420

Zinfandel,'91, Arroyo Grande Vly., Estate $12.00 (3)

SAUSAL WINERY

7370 Hwy. 128 Healdsburg 95448

Cabernet Sauvignon,'88, Alexander Vly. $14.00 (B-State Fair)

SCHARFFENBERGER

307 Talmadge Rd. Ukiah 95482

Sparkling Wine,'NV, Mendocino Co., Brut $19.00 (S-Orange)

SCHRAMSBERG

1400 Schramsberg Rd. Calistoga 94515

Sparkling Wine,'88, Napa Vly., Blanc de Blancs $22.25 (B-Orange)
Sparkling Wine,'89, Napa Vly., Cuvee Du Pinot $22.25 (B-Orange)

SCHUG CELLARS

6204 St. Helena Hwy. Yountville 94599

Pinot Noir,'89, Carneros, Beckstoffer Vnyd. $13.00 (B-San Diego)
Pinot Noir,'90, Carneros, Beckstoffer Vnyd. $13.00 (B-State Fair)

SEBASTIANI VINEYARDS

389 Fourth St. E. Sonoma 95476

Cabernet Franc,'89, Sonoma Co., Family Selection $9.00 (3)
Cabernet Sauvignon,'88, Sonoma Co., Reserve $14.00 (4)
Cabernet Sauvignon,'89, Sonoma Series $9.00 (3)
Cabernet Sauvignon,'89, Sonoma Vly., Cherryblock (3)
Cabernet Sauvignon,'91, California (B-W. Coast)

Chardonnay,'91, Sonoma Co., Reserve (3)
Chardonnay,'91, Sonoma Series $9.00 (3)
Merlot,'90, Sonoma Co. (3)
Merlot,'91, Sonoma Co. $9.00 (4)
Red Meritage,'89, Sonoma, Red Hill Vineyard $14.00 (3)
Zinfandel,'89, Sonoma Series $9.00 (3)
Zinfandel,'90, Sonoma Series $9.00 (B-L.A.)

SEGHESIO WINERY
14730 Grove St. Healdsburg 95448
Cabernet Sauvignon,'91, Sonoma Co. $10.00 (G-L.A.)
Chardonnay,'91, Sonoma Co. (B-W. Coast)
Sauvignon Blanc,'92, Dry Creek Vly. $8.00 (2)
Zinfandel,'91, Sonoma Co. $8.00 (4)

SEQUOIA GROVE VINEYARDS
8338 St. Helena Hwy. Napa 94558
Cabernet Sauvignon,'89, Napa Vly. $16.00 (6)
Cabernet Sauvignon,'89, Napa Vly., Reserve $25.00 (S-Dallas)
Cabernet Sauvignon,'90, Napa Vly, Estate $16.00 (2)
Cabernet Sauvignon,'90, Napa Vly., Estate Reserve $25.00 (3)
Chardonnay,'90, Napa Vly., Estate $16.00 (6)
Chardonnay,'91, Napa Vly., Carneros $14.00 (2)

SHADOW MOUNTAIN
1500 Ruddick Cunningham Talmage 95481
Chardonnay,'92, California $7.00 (B-Orange)

SHAFER VINEYARDS
6154 Silverado Trail Napa 94558
Cabernet Sauvignon,'89, Napa Vly. (B-Dallas)
Cabernet Sauvignon,'89, Stags Leap, Hillside Sel. $35.00 (S-San
Cabernet Sauvignon,'90, Napa Vly., Stag's Leap Dist. $19.00 (4)
Chardonnay,'91, Napa Vly., Barrel Select $15.00 (3)
Merlot,'91, Napa Vly. $20.00 (4)

SHENANDOAH VINEYARDS
12300 Steiner Rd. Plymouth 95669
Cabernet Sauvignon,'90, Amador Co. $8.00 (B-Orange)
Sauvignon Blanc,'91, Amador Co. $7.00 (B-Orange)

SIERRA VISTA WINERY
4560 Cabernet Way Placerville 95667
Sauvignon Blanc,'92, El Dorado $7.50 (2)

SILVER CANYON
Address Not Available
Cabernet Sauvignon,'89, Paso Robles (2)

SILVER RIDGE VINEYARDS
Address Not Available
Cabernet Sauvignon,'89, Napa Vly. (2)
Chardonnay,'91, California, Barrel Ferm. $12.00 (6)

SILVERADO HILL CELLARS
3105 Silverado Trail Napa 94558
Chardonnay,'91, Napa Vly., Special Release (B-State Fair)

SILVERADO VINEYARDS
6121 Silverado Trail Napa 94558
Cabernet Sauvignon,'90, Stags Leap Dist. $16.50 (5)

Cabernet Sauvignon,'90, Stags Leap, Res. $40.00 (S-San Fran)
Merlot,'90, Stag's Leap Dist. $16.50 (2)
Sauvignon Blanc,'91, Napa Vly. (B-San Diego)
Sauvignon Blanc,'92, Napa Vly. (2)

SIMI WINERY
16275 Healdsburg Ave. Healdsburg 95448

Cabernet Sauvignon,'89, Alexander Vly. $15.00 (B-Dallas)
Chardonnay,'90, Mendocino/Sonoma/Napa $12.00 (2)
Chardonnay,'91, Sonoma/Mendocino/Napa $12.00 (2)
Chenin Blanc,'90, Mendocino Co. $7.00 (B-Dallas)
Chenin Blanc,'91, Mendocino Co. $7.00 (3)
Sauvignon Blanc,'91, Sonoma Co. $9.00 (B-San Diego)

SINGLE LEAF VINEYARDS
Address Not Available

Zinfandel,'90, El Dorado (B-W. Coast)

ROBERT SINSKEY VINEYARDS
6320 Silverado Trail Napa 94558

Merlot,'90, Napa Vly., Los Carneros $19.00 (S-State Fair)
Pinot Noir,'91, Napa Vly., Los Carneros $19.00 (2)

SMITH & HOOK WINERY
37700 Foothill Rd. Soledad 93960

Merlot,'89, Santa Lucia Highlands $15.00 (S-San Fran)

SMITH VINEYARD
13719 Dog Bar Road Grass Valley 95949

Chenin Blanc,'91, Sierra Foothills, Estate $3.89 (B-Orange)

SMITH-MADRONE
4022 Spring Mountain Rd. St Helena 94574

Johannisberg Riesling,'92, Napa $9.00 (B-San Fran)

SOBON ESTATE
14430 Shenandoah Rd. Plymouth 95669

Zinfandel,'90, Sierra Foothills (B-State Fair)

SOLITUDE
Address Not Available

Chardonnay,'91, Carneros, Sangiacomo Vnyd. $18.00 (S-Orange)

SONOMA CREEK WINERY
23355 Millerick Road Sonoma 95476

Cabernet Sauvignon,'90, Sonoma Vly. $10.00 (3)
Cabernet Sauvignon,'91, Sonoma Co. $10.00 (2)
Chardonnay,'91, Carneros, Barrel Ferm. $11.00 (2)
Zinfandel,'91, Sonoma Vly. (2)

SONOMA MISSION WINERY
600 Addison Street Berkeley 94710

Chardonnay,'91, Sonoma Co. (G-State Fair)

SONORA WINERY
P. O. Box 242 Sonora 95370

Zinfandel,'90, Sonoma, Passalacqua Vnyd. $9.00 (S-Dallas)
Zinfandel,'91, Amador Co., TC Vnyd. $9.00 (B-San Diego)

SOQUEL VINEYARDS
Address Not Available

Cabernet Sauvignon,'90, Santa Cruz Mtns. $16.00 (B-San Fran)

ST. ANDREWS WINERY
2921 Silverado Trail   Napa   94558
Chardonnay,'91, Napa Vly. (B-State Fair)
Sauvignon Blanc,'92, Napa Vly. (S-State Fair)

ST. CLEMENT VINEYARDS
2867 St. Helena Hwy. N.   St Helena   94574
Cabernet Sauvignon,'89, Napa Vly. $20.00 (3)
Cabernet Sauvignon,'90, Napa Vly. $20.00 (4)
Chardonnay,'90, Napa, Carneros $16.00 (B-W. Coast)
Chardonnay,'91, Carneros, Abbotts Vnyd. (B-San Diego)
Chardonnay,'91, Napa Vly. $16.00 (2)
Merlot,'90, Napa Vly. $20.00 (5)
Sauvignon Blanc,'92, Napa Vly. $10.50 (5)

ST. FRANCIS WINERY
8450 Sonoma Hwy.   Kenwood   95452
Cabernet Sauvignon,'89, Sonoma Vly., Reserve $24.00 (2)
Cabernet Sauvignon,'90, Sonoma, Reserve $24.00 (B-San Fran)
Chardonnay,'91, Sonoma Vly., Reserve $15.00 (3)
Merlot,'90, Sonoma Vly. $17.00 (2)
Merlot,'90, Sonoma Vly., Estate Reserve $24.00 (B-San Fran)

ST. SUPERY WINERY
P. O. Box 38   Rutherford   94573
Cabernet Sauvignon,'89, Napa Vly., Dollarhide Ranch (3)
Chardonnay,'91, Napa Vly., Dollarhide Ranch $12.50 (3)
Merlot,'90, Napa Vly., Dollarhide Ranch (4)
Sauvignon Blanc,'91, Napa Vly., Dollarhide Ranch $9.00 (3)

STAG'S LEAP WINE CELLARS
5766 Silverado Trail   Napa   94558
Cabernet Sauvignon,'89, Stag's Leap, Fay Vnyd. $27.00 (B-San
Cabernet Sauvignon,'90, Napa Vly. $18.00 (2)
Chardonnay,'91, Napa Vly. $18.00 (2)

STAGLIN FAMILY VINEYARD
Address Not Available
Cabernet Sauvignon,'90, Napa Vly. $25.00 (S-Orange)

STELTZNER VINEYARDS
5998 Silverado Trail   Napa   94558
Cabernet Sauvignon,'88, Napa Vly. (2)
Merlot,'91, Napa Vly., Stags Leap, Estate $17.00 (G-Orange)

ROBERT STEMMLER WINERY
3805 Lambert Bridge Rd.   Healdsburg   95448
Pinot Noir,'89, Sonoma Co. $20.00 (2)

STERLING VINEYARDS
1111 Dunaweal Ln.   Calistoga   94515
Cabernet Sauvignon,'90, Napa Vly. (B-W. Coast)
Chardonnay,'89, Napa, Diamond Mt. Ranch $18.00 (2)
Merlot,'90, Napa Vly., Estate $14.00 (S-Orange)
Red Meritage,'88, Three Palms Vnyd. $23.00 (B-State Fair)
Red Meritage,'89, Napa Vly. Reserve $40.00 (S-Farmers)

STEVENOT WINERY
2690 San Domingo Rd.   Murphys   95247
Cabernet Sauvignon,'89, Calaveras Co., Reserve (2)

Chardonnay,'91, Calaveras Co., Reserve $10.00 (G-State Fair)
Zinfandel,'89, Amador Co., LH (B-State Fair)
Zinfandel,'89, California (S-State Fair)

STONE CELLARS
Address Not Available
Zinfandel,'90, Napa Vly. (S-State Fair)

STONE CREEK CELLARS
539 Broadway #D Sonoma 95476
Cabernet Sauvignon,'86, Napa, Special Sel. (B-San Diego)
Cabernet Sauvignon,'89, California (B-New World)
Chardonnay,'89, North Coast (S-New World)
Chardonnay,'90, Alexander Vly. (B-State Fair)
Chardonnay,'91, California (2)
Merlot,'91, California, Special Selection $6.25 (3)
Sauvignon Blanc,'91, Napa, Fume, Special Sel. $6.25 (2)
White Zinfandel,'92, California $5.50 (2)

J. STONESTREET & SONS
337 Healdsburg Ave. Healdsburg 94558
Cabernet Sauvignon,'90, Alexander Vly. $24.00 (B-State Fair)
Chardonnay,'90, Sonoma Co. $20.00 (6)
Merlot,'89, Alexander Vly. (S-State Fair)
Pinot Noir,'91, Russian River Vly. $30.00 (2)

STONY RIDGE WINERY
4948 Tesla Road Livermore 94550
Cabernet Sauvignon,'91, California $6.50 (S-Farmers)
Chardonnay,'91, California Collection $6.50 (2)
Johannisberg Riesling,'92, Monterey Co., Ltd. Release $5.50 (2)
Merlot,'91, North Coast, Ltd. Release $9.00 (4)

STORRS WINERY
303 Potrero St. #35 Santa Cruz 95060
Chardonnay,'91, Ben Lomond, Beauregard (G-Dallas)
Chardonnay,'91, Santa Cruz Mtns. (3)
Chardonnay,'91, Santa Cruz Mtns., Dirk Vnyd. $16.00 (B-Orange)
Chardonnay,'91, Santa Cruz Mtns., Meyley Vnyd. $18.00 (2)
Gewurztraminer,'92, Monterey Viento Vnyd. $9.00 (3)
Petite Sirah,'91, Santa Cruz Mtns. $14.00 (3)

STORYBOOK MT. VINEYARDS
3835 Hwy. 128 Calistoga 94515
Zinfandel,'88, Napa Vly., Reserve $19.50 (2)
Zinfandel,'89, Napa Vly., Estate Reserve $19.50 (2)
Zinfandel,'90, Napa Vly. $13.50 (B-Farmers)
Zinfandel,'91, Napa Vly. $14.00 (G-San Fran)

RODNEY STRONG VINEYARDS
11455 Old Redwood Hwy. Windsor 95492
Cabernet Sauvignon,'90, Sonoma Co. $10.00 (3)
Chardonnay,'91, Chalk Hill Vnyd. (G-L.A.)
Chardonnay,'92, Sonoma Co. $9.00 (2)
Pinot Noir,'91, River East Vnyd. $14.00 (5)
Sauvignon Blanc,'92, Charlotte's Home Vnyd. $9.00 (2)
Zinfandel,'90, River West, Old Vines Vnyd. $14.00 (3)

SUMMIT LAKE VINEYARDS
2000 Summit Lake Dr. Angwin 94508
Zinfandel,'89, Howell Mtn. (B-State Fair)

SUNRISE
13100 Montebello Rd. Cupertino 95014
Cabernet Sauvignon,'88, Santa Cruz Mtns. $15.00 (3)
Chardonnay,'91, Livermore Vly., Beyers Ranch $10.00 (2)
Pinot Noir,'89, Santa Clara, San Ysidro Vnyd. $15.00 (B-Orange)
Zinfandel,'90, Santa Cruz, Picchetti Ranch (S-L.A.)

SUTTER HOME
277 St. Helena Hwy. So. St Helena 94574
Chardonnay,'91, California $5.95 (3)
Chenin Blanc,'92, California $4.45 (B-Orange)
White Zinfandel,'92, California (B-W. Coast)
Zinfandel,'89, Amador Co., Reserve (B-State Fair)

SWANSON VINEYARDS
1271 Manley Lane Rutherford 94573
Cabernet Sauvignon,'88, Napa Vly. $23.00 (3)
Cabernet Sauvignon,'89, Napa Vly. $23.00 (5)
Chardonnay,'90, Napa Vly, Estate Reserve $20.00 (2)
Chardonnay,'90, Napa Vly., Estate $16.00 (4)
Merlot,'90, Napa Vly., Estate $15.00 (2)
Semillon,'89, Napa Vly., LH $50.00 (2)
Zinfandel,'88, Napa Vly. $12.00 (3)
Zinfandel,'89, Napa Vly. $12.00 (B-L.A.)

SYLVESTER VINEYARDS
Address Not Available
Cabernet Sauvignon,'88, Paso Robles, Kiara Reserve $9.00 (4)

T

TAFT STREET WINERY
6450 First St. Forestville 95436
Chardonnay,'91, Sonoma Co. $8.00 (4)
Merlot,'91, Sonoma $11.00 (B-San Fran)
Sauvignon Blanc,'91, Sonoma Co. $6.00 (5)

TALLEY VINEYARDS
3031 Lopez Drive Arroyo Grande 93420
Chardonnay,'91, Arroyo Grande Vly., Estate $16.00 (S-Orange)

TAN TAMAS WINES
5565 Tesla Road Livermore 94550
Chardonnay,'91, Livermore Vly., Hayes Ranch (S-New World)

TANBARK HILL VINEYARD
P. O. Box 81 St Helena 94574
Cabernet Sauvignon,'88, Napa Vly. $23.00 (S-Orange)

TIN PONY
9786 Ross Station Road Sebastopol 95472
Sauvignon Blanc,'91, Alexander Vly., Barrel Ferm. $9.00 (S-Orange)

TITUS
Address Not Available
Cabernet Sauvignon,'90, Napa Vly. $20.00 (2)

TIVOLI
1473 Yountville Cross Rd. Yountville 94599
Sparkling Wine,'NV, Napa Vly., Brut Noir $10.00 (G-Orange)

TOPAZ WINES
1937 Waverly Street Napa 94558
Red Meritage,'90, Napa Vly, Rouge de Trois $16.00 (G-Orange)

TOPOLOS AT RUSSIAN RIVER VINEYARDS
5700 Gravenstein Hwy., No. Forestville 95436
Chardonnay,'92, Sonoma Mtn., Barrel Ferm. $12.00 (S-Orange)
Zinfandel,'90, Sonoma Co. $8.50 (S-Dallas)
Zinfandel,'91, Sonoma Co. $8.50 (3)
Zinfandel,'91, Sonoma Co., Rossi Ranch, Old Vines $14.50 (2)

TOURELLE
Address Not Available
Cabernet Sauvignon,'89, Napa Vly. $14.00 (S-San Fran)

TRADER JOE'S
538 Mission St. South Pasadena 91030
Merlot,'92, Napa Vly., President's Reserve $5.00 (S-Orange)

TREFETHEN VINEYARDS
1160 Oak Knoll Ave. Napa 94558
Chardonnay,'90, Napa Vly., Estate $18.00 (S-San Fran)
Johannisberg Riesling,'91, Napa Vly., Estate $9.25 (B-San Diego)
Johannisberg Riesling,'92, Napa Vly., White $9.25 (S-State Fair)

TRELLIS VINEYARDS
Address Not Available
Chardonnay,'92, Sonoma Co. (S-State Fair)

TRENTADUE
19170 Redwood Hwy. Geyserville 95441
Chardonnay,'91, Alexander Vly. $9.00 (2)
Merlot,'91, Alexander Vly. $10.00 (S-State Fair)
Petite Sirah,'91, Sonoma Co. $11.00 (3)
Zinfandel,'90, Alexander Vly. $10.00 (4)

TRINITY
Address Not Available
Sparkling Wine,'NV, California, Brut (B-New World)

TROUT GULCH VINEYARDS
18426 Chelmsford Dr. Cupertino 95014
Chardonnay,'90, Santa Cruz Mtns. $14.00 (4)
Chardonnay,'91, Santa Cruz Mtns. $14.00 (S-State Fair)
Pinot Noir,'90, Santa Cruz Mtns. $20.00 (2)

TRUCHARD VINEYARDS
3234 Old Sonoma Rd. Napa 94559
Cabernet Sauvignon,'89, Napa Vly. (B-W. Coast)
Merlot,'90, Napa Vly. (2)
Pinot Noir,'91, Napa Vly. (2)

TRUCKEE RIVER WINERY
1117 Torrey Pine Truckee 96161
Pinot Noir,'90, Carneros (B-State Fair)

TULOCAY WINERY
1426 Coombsville   Napa   94558
Cabernet Sauvignon,'87, Napa Vly., Cliff Vnyd. (2)
Chardonnay,'89, Napa Vly., de Celles Vnyd. $13.00 (B-Farmers)

TWIN HILLS RANCH WINERY
2025 Lake Nacimiento Dr.   Paso Robles   93447
Cabernet Sauvignon,'89, Paso Robles, Estate (B-San Diego)
Johannisberg Riesling,'NV, Paso Robles $7.25 (B-Farmers)
White Zinfandel,'NV, Paso Robles Rose $5.50 (2)

V

A. G. VALLEJO WINERY
1883 London Ranch Rd.   Glen Ellen   95442
Chardonnay,'91, California $6.00 (S-New World)
Chardonnay,'92, California $6.00 (S-State Fair)
Merlot,'91, California Harvest Select $7.50 (2)
Sauvignon Blanc,'91, California $6.00 (S-New World)
White Zinfandel,'92, Calif., Harvest Select $6.00 (7)

VALLEY OF THE MOON WINERY
777 Madrona Rd.   Glen Ellen   95442
Cabernet Sauvignon,'89, Sonoma Co. $9.00 (2)
White Zinfandel,'92, California $6.00 (S-Orange)

VALLEY RIDGE
539 Broadway #D   Sonoma   95476
Cabernet Sauvignon,'89, Sonoma Co. (S-New World)
Chardonnay,'89, Sonoma Co. (S-New World)
Merlot,'91, Sonoma Co. $9.00 (5)
Sauvignon Blanc,'91, Sonoma Co. $6.00 (S-Orange)

VAN DER HEYDEN VINEYARDS
4057 Silverado Trail   Napa   94558
Cabernet Sauvignon,'89, Napa. $18.00 (G-San Fran)
Cabernet Sauvignon,'90, Napa Vly., LH (B-San Diego)

VAN DER KAMP CHAMPAGNE
307 Warm Springs Rd.   Kenwood   95452
Sparkling Wine,'87, Sonoma Vly., English Cuvee $14.50 (B-Dallas)
Sparkling Wine,'88, Sonoma Vly., Brut $14.50 (7)
Sparkling Wine,'89, Sonoma Vly., Midnight Cuvee $14.50 (5)

VENDANGE
389 4th St. E.   Sonoma   95476
Cabernet Sauvignon,'91, California $6.00 (3)
Merlot,'91, California $6.00 (2)
Merlot,'92, California $6.00 (B-L.A.)
White Zinfandel,'92, California $6.00 (3)

VENTANA VINEYARDS
2999 Monterey Salinas Hwy.   Monterey   93940
Chardonnay,'89, Monterey, Eagle, Estate $16.00 (2)
Chardonnay,'90, Monterey, Crystal, Barrel Ferm. (2)
Chardonnay,'90, Monterey, Gold Stripe Sel. $10.00 (2)
Chardonnay,'91, Monterey, Gold Stripe $10.00 (S-L.A.)
Chenin Blanc,'91, Monterey Co. (B-San Diego)
Johannisberg Riesling,'91, Monterey, Estate $6.00 (2)
Sauvignon Blanc,'91, Monterey Co., Estate $8.00 (2)

Semillon,'89, Monterey (S-New World)
Syrah,'91, Monterey $9.00 (B-San Fran)

VIADER
P. O. Box 280 Deer Park 94576
Red Meritage,'90, Napa Vly. $25.00 (G-Orange)

VICHON WINERY
1595 Oakville Grade Oakville 94562
Cabernet Sauvignon,'89, Calif., Coastal Sel. $9.00 (B-Orange)
Cabernet Sauvignon,'89, Stags Leap Dist. $24.00 (3)
Cabernet Sauvignon,'90, Calif., Coastal Selection $9.00 (2)
Cabernet Sauvignon,'90, Napa Vly. (3)
Chardonnay,'90, Napa Vly. $15.00 (S-San Diego)
Chardonnay,'91, California, Coastal Selection $9.00 (2)
Chardonnay,'91, Napa Vly. $15.00 (3)
Red Meritage,'89, Napa Vly., Estate $34.00 (S-San Fran)
White Meritage,'91, Napa Vly., Chevrignon $9.60 (4)

VILLA MT. EDEN WINERY
620 Oakville Cross Rd. Oakville 94562
Cabernet Sauvignon,'88, Napa Vly., Reserve $15.00 (G-Farmers)
Cabernet Sauvignon,'89, Napa Vly., Grand Reserve $15.00 (5)
Cabernet Sauvignon,'90, California, Cellar Select $10.00 (5)
Chardonnay,'91, California, Cellar Select $10.00 (4)
Chardonnay,'91, Carneros, Grand Reserve $15.00 (3)
Merlot,'90, Napa Vly., Grand Reserve $15.00 (6)
Pinot Noir,'91, Grand Reserve $15.00 (B-L.A.)
Zinfandel,'91, California, Cellar Select $10.00 (4)

VINA VISTA WINERY
14401 Chianti Road Geyserville 95441
Cabernet Sauvignon,'88, Alexander Vly. $12.00 (3)
Merlot,'90, Alexander Vly. $12.00 (B-Farmers)

VINEYARD HILL
Address Not Available
Chardonnay,'91, Mendocino Co. $5.00 (B-Orange)

VON STRASSER
1510 Diamond Mtn. Road Calistoga 94515
Cabernet Sauvignon,'90, Diamond Mtn. $25.00 (B-Orange)

VOSS VINEYARDS
Address Not Available
Zinfandel,'91, Alexander Vly. (G-New World)

W

WARNER WEST
Address Not Available
Johannisberg Riesling,'90, Santa Barbara Co., LH $9.95 (S-Orange)
Johannisberg Riesling,'91, Santa Barbara, Res. $7.95 (B-Orange)

WEIBEL VINEYARDS
1250 Stanford Ave. Mission San Jose 94538
Cabernet Sauvignon,'89, Mendocino Co. $5.00 (B-Orange)
Cabernet Sauvignon,'89, Mendocino, Reserve $8.00 (3)
Sparkling Wine,'NV, California, Spumante $4.00 (B-Orange)

WELLINGTON VINEYARDS
P. O. Box 568 Glen Ellen 95442
Cabernet Sauvignon,'89, Sonoma, Mohrhardt Ridge (B-San
Cabernet Sauvignon,'90, Sonoma, Mohrhardt Ridge (B-San
Red Meritage,'89, Napa Vly. Mt. Veeder District $20.00 (B-Farmers)
Zinfandel,'90, Sonoma Vly., Old Vines (S-New World)

WENTE BROS.
5565 Tesla Road Livermore 94550
Cabernet Sauvignon,'90, Livermore Vly., Estate $9.00 (2)
Chardonnay,'91, Arroyo Seco, Riva Ranch Vnyd. $14.00 (2)
Chardonnay,'91, Livermore Vly., Estate Reserve $16.00 (2)
Chardonnay,'92, Central Coast $8.00 (S-State Fair)
Johannisberg Riesling,'89, Arroyo Seco, LH $20.00 (6)
Merlot,'91, Livermore Vly., Crane Ridge $14.00 (5)
Semillon,'91, Livermore Vly., Estate $8.00 (5)
Sparkling Wine,'82, Arroyo Seco, Res., Brut (B-San Diego)
Sparkling Wine,'NV, Arroyo Seco, Grande Brut $10.00 (3)

WESTWOOD WINERY
1709 Carson Road Placerville 95667
Pinot Noir,'89, Napa Vly., Haynes Vnyd., Res. (B-New World)
Pinot Noir,'90, Napa Vly., Haynes Vnyd. (2)
Pinot Noir,'91, California $10.00 (2)

WILLIAM WHEELER WINERY
130 Plaza Street Healdsburg 95448
Cabernet Sauvignon,'89, Dry Creek Vly. $12.50 (2)
Chardonnay,'91, Sonoma Co. (B-San Diego)
Chardonnay,'91, Sonoma, Norse Sel., Barrel Ferm. (B-San Diego)
Zinfandel,'91, Dry Creek Vly. $12.00 (S-Orange)

WHITE OAK VINEYARDS
208 Haydon St. Healdsburg 95448
Chardonnay,'90, Sonoma Co., Myers Reserve $20.00 (B-Farmers)
Chardonnay,'91, Sonoma Co. $12.95 (3)
Chenin Blanc,'91, California $6.95 (B-Farmers)
Sauvignon Blanc,'92, Sonoma Co. $8.95 (2)
Zinfandel,'91, Sonoma $9.00 (3)
Zinfandel,'91, Sonoma Co., Ltd. Reserve $12.95 (2)

WHITE ROCK VINEYARDS
1115 Loma Vista Dr. Napa 94558
Chardonnay,'91, Napa Vly. $16.00 (G-San Fran)

WHITEHALL LANE WINERY
1563 St. Helena Hwy. St Helena 94574
Cabernet Franc,'90, Napa Vly. $15.00 (4)
Cabernet Sauvignon,'88, Napa Vly., Reserve (S-Dallas)
Cabernet Sauvignon,'89, Napa Vly., Reserve (2)
Cabernet Sauvignon,'90, Napa Vly. $15.00 (B-W. Coast)
Merlot,'90, Knights Vly., Summers Ranch $14.00 (G-Orange)

WHITFORD CELLARS
4047 E. Third Avenue Napa 94558
Chardonnay,'90, Napa Vly., Haynes Vnyd. (2)

WILD HOG HILL WINES
Address Not Available
Pinot Noir,'90, Sonoma $11.00 (B-San Fran)

WILD HOG VINEYARD
P. O. Box 189 Cazadero 95421
Pinot Noir,'91, Sonoma, Estate, Organic $11.00 (B-San Fran)

WILD HORSE WINERY
P. O. Box 638 Templeton 93465
Cabernet Sauvignon,'90, Paso Robles $12.00 (2)
Chardonnay,'91, Central Coast $14.00 (S-San Fran)
Chardonnay,'92, Central Coast $14.00 (3)
Merlot,'90, Central Coast $14.00 (3)
Merlot,'91, Central Coast $15.00 (B-San Fran)
Pinot Blanc,'92, Monterey $12.00 (B-Orange)
Pinot Noir,'91, Central Coast $16.00 (4)
Syrah,'90, Paso Robles (B-State Fair)
Zinfandel,'89, Paso Robles (G-State Fair)
Zinfandel,'90, Paso Robles (2)

WILDHURST VINEYARDS
11171 Highway 29 Lower Lake 95457
Chardonnay,'91, Sonoma Co. $11.00 (2)
Merlot,'91, Clear Lake $11.00 (3)
Sauvignon Blanc,'91, Clear Lake $9.00 (B-San Fran)
White Meritage,'91, Clear Lake Matillaha $16.00 (2)

J. WILE & SONS
401 So. St. Helena Hwy. St Helena 94574
Cabernet Sauvignon,'91, Napa Vly. $10.00 (2)
Chardonnay,'91, Napa Vly. (B-New World)
Merlot,'90, Napa Vly. $7.00 (3)

WINDEMERE WINES
Address Not Available
Cabernet Sauvignon,'90, Napa Vly., Diamond Mtn. (2)

WINDSOR VINEYARDS
11455 Old Redwood Hwy. Healdsburg 95448
Cabernet Sauvignon,'88, North Coast $12.00 (2)
Cabernet Sauvignon,'88, River West Vnyd., Estate $13.00 (2)
Cabernet Sauvignon,'88, Sonoma Co., Signature Series (B-Dallas)
Cabernet Sauvignon,'89, Sonoma Co. $10.00 (2)
Cabernet Sauvignon,'89, Sonoma Co., Signature Series $18.00 (4)
Cabernet Sauvignon,'90, Mendocino Co., Reserve $14.50 (3)
Chardonnay,'90, Murphy Ranch (S-L.A.)
Chardonnay,'91, Alexander Vly., Murphy Ranch (B-San Diego)
Chardonnay,'91, Russian River Vly., Reserve $14.00 (2)
Chardonnay,'91, Russian River, Preston Ranch (2)
Chardonnay,'91, Sonoma Co. (B-L.A.)
Chardonnay,'91, Sonoma, Signature Series $20.00 (4)
Chenin Blanc,'92, Alexander Vly. $7.00 (3)
Gewurztraminer,'92, Alexander Vly. $7.00 (6)
Johannisberg Riesling,'91, Winemaster's Sel. $7.50 (B-Orange)
Johannisberg Riesling,'92, LeBaron Vnyd. $7.50 (5)
Merlot,'89, Sonoma Co., Winemaster Sel. (B-San Diego)
Merlot,'90, Russian River Vly. (2)
Petite Sirah,'90, North Coast $10.00 (3)
Petite Sirah,'NV, Sonoma Co. $9.50 (2)
Pinot Noir,'90, Russian River Vly. $10.00 (6)
Sauvignon Blanc,'92, Sonoma Co., Fume $7.50 (3)

Sparkling Wine,'88, Sonoma Co., Blanc de Blanc $17.50 (6)
Sparkling Wine,'88, Sonoma Co., Blanc de Noir $13.33 (6)
Sparkling Wine,'88, Sonoma Co., Brut Rose $12.00 (5)
Sparkling Wine,'NV, California, Extra Dry (G-State Fair)
White Zinfandel,'92, Sonoma Co. $7.00 (2)
Zinfandel,'90, Alexander Vly., Reserve $12.00 (3)
Zinfandel,'90, Sonoma $8.00 (G-San Fran)
Zinfandel,'90, Sonoma Co., Reserve $10.00 (2)
Zinfandel,'90, Sonoma Co., Signature Series (2)

WINDWALKER VINEYARDS
7360 Perry Creek Somerset 95684
Chenin Blanc,'92, El Dorado, Dry (S-State Fair)

WINTERBROOK WINERY
4851 Buena Vista Road Ione 95640
Cabernet Sauvignon,'90, Napa Vly., Grand Reserve $15.00 (2)
Chardonnay,'91, Napa Vly., Grand Reserve (B-State Fair)
Zinfandel,'91, Sonoma Co. (S-State Fair)

WOODBRIDGE
4614 W. Turner Rd. Lodi 95640
Cabernet Sauvignon,'90, California (B-New World)
Chardonnay,'91, California (S-New World)
Chenin Blanc,'91, California $4.50 (G-Orange)
Sauvignon Blanc,'91, California $4.75 (B-Orange)
Zinfandel,'90, California $7.00 (Σ-New World)

WOODEN VALLEY WINERY
4756 Suisun Valley Rd. Suisun 94585
Chardonnay,'NV, Suisun Vly. (S-State Fair)

WOODSIDE VINEYARDS
340 Kings Mtn. Road Woodside 94062
Chardonnay,'91, Santa Cruz Mtns., Estate $16.00 (2)

Y

YORK MOUNTAIN WINERY
Rt. 2, Box 191 Templeton 93465
Cabernet Sauvignon,'87, San Luis Obispo Co. (3)
Cabernet Sauvignon,'88, San Luis Obispo Co. $12.00 (2)
Merlot,'90, San Luis Obispo Co. $12.00 (B-Orange)

Z

ZACA MESA WINERY
Foxen Canyon Rd. Los Olivos 93441
Chardonnay,'90, Santa Barbara Co., Reserve $16.50 (3)
Chardonnay,'91, Santa Barbara Co. $11.00 (2)
Pinot Noir,'90, Santa Barbara Co., Reserve $16.00 (4)
Syrah,'90, Santa Barbara Co. $12.00 (B-New World)
Syrah,'91, Santa Barbara Co. $12.00 (5)

ZD WINES
8383 Silverado Trail Napa 94558
Cabernet Sauvignon,'90, Napa Vly. $20.00 (7)
Chardonnay,'91, California $20.50 (4)
Pinot Noir,'91, Napa Vly., Carneros $17.00 (2)

STEPHEN ZELLERBACH VINEYARD
4611 Thomas Road Healdsburg 95448
Cabernet Sauvignon,'89, California, Robert Alison (G-San Diego)
Chardonnay,'91, Sonoma Co. $8.00 (B-Orange)